Vindolanda

NEW ASPECTS OF ANTIQUITY

Edited by the late Sir Mortimer Wheeler

Vindolanda

A Roman frontier post on Hadrian's Wall

Robin Birley

15 colour plates
84 monochrome plates
45 line drawings

T & H

THAMES AND HUDSON

For Eric Birley

*Colour illustrations originated by
Adroit Photo Litho, Birmingham and printed by
Jolly and Barber Limited, Rugby, Great Britain
Monochrome illustrations and text filmset
and printed in Great Britain by
BAS Printers Limited, Wallop, Hampshire*

Contents

General editor's preface

It is apposite that the title-page of a monograph on Vindolanda should bear the name of the dynasty of Birley a trifle possessively as its *signum*. It is an age-long tradition that the Emperor Hadrian's successors should share with the great builder something of the status which attaches to long lines of owners, geographers, historians and archaeologists who have combined in one way or another to commemorate the vestiges of his great frontier. Vindolanda, alias Chesterholm, is in this book chosen as a pivotal site which has drawn particularly rewarding enquiry from a wide range of investigators since one Christopher Hunter, a physician from Durham City, in 1702 contributed an account of its remains to *Philosophical Transactions*; or since the Revd John Horsley in *Britannia Romana* (London 1732) published some inscriptions including one which enabled him to show that the site was that of the Vindolana of the *Notitia Dignitatum* (see p. 26). In 1769 John Wallis in his *Natural History of Northumberland* was able to add evidence of a substantial civilian settlement west of the visible fort.

But it may be said that the systematic archaeology of the site began in 1929, when Eric Birley, father of the author of this report, was able to acquire it at the sale of the Clayton estate. Excavations ensued in 1930, in time for the new owner to describe something of the possibilities of the fort and its annex to the considerable body of appreciative scholars who that year constituted the distinguished 'Pilgrimage' to the Wall and its environs, on the model initiated by John Collingwood Bruce as long previously as 1849 with a view to popularizing the works of the Wall. I well remember Birley intimating on that occasion in 1930 that his endeavours would encompass not merely the military remains but their civilian counterparts as well, for the *vicani*, he rightly maintained, had been too long neglected. However, after many fruitful years' enquiry within the fort walls, at east, north and west gateways and in the headquarters building, Birley had to postpone any substantive research amongst the civilian ruins in favour of a prolonged period of excavation not 2 miles distant at Housesteads, that imposing Hadrianic edifice on the Wall.

But the *vicani Vindolandesses* were not to remain neglected and forgotten. Soon Robin Birley, following in his distinguished father's footsteps, was developing the reasoned processes of critical investigation in practice-soundings beyond the fort walls. Trial sections in 1949, 1956 and 1959 merely whetted his youthful appetite; preliminary probings within the civilian settlement between 1967 and 1969 proved beyond the shadow of a doubt the existence here of substantial and largely undisturbed civilian structures, so that when the opportunity for full-scale investigation presented itself in 1970 in the shape of the Vindolanda Trust under the benevolent patronage of Mrs Daphne Archibald, young Birley was ready and prepared for the major burden of research that lay ahead.

It is to these recent and important researches, under the continuous and continuing guidance of the Birley family, that the present report in the main devotes itself.

1976   MORTIMER WHEELER

Foreword and acknowledgments

The excavations at Vindolanda have been made possible by the enthusiastic support of many thousands of visitors, for whom the north-western frontier of the Roman empire is still a place to marvel at. This book is for them. It attempts to place the work at Vindolanda in its context as part of the whole research programme into the northern Roman frontier in Britain, and it serves as a summary report on the first six years' excavations.

The fort and civilian settlement at Vindolanda had a long and complicated history during the Roman period, stretching back to the time before Hadrian's Wall was built. I have tried in this book to explain the sequence of occupation and to convey something of the sheer wealth of material that has been discovered so far and how it affects our understanding of the civilians of Vindolanda, the *vicani Vindolandesses*. Inevitably the remarkable cache of pre-Hadrianic writing tablets looms large in the story, but coins, altars, statuettes, gemstones, textiles, leather, pottery and all kinds of organic remains bear witness to the fertility of the site as a whole. Some of our hypotheses regarding Roman building methods were tested in full-scale replicas of sections of Hadrian's Stone and Turf Walls. Other, new theories suggested by the recent excavations, however, must await future research for proof.

A large excavation in any country is a complicated operation, demanding the time and skills of a host of people and the never-ending search for funds. The work at Vindolanda would not have been possible without the support of many organizations and private individuals, too numerous to mention here. Of crucial value in the first three years was a grant from the Sir James Knott Trust and assistance from the English Tourist Board. The *Observer* newspaper aided our excavation budget in 1973, while BP Chemicals Ltd made a valuable contribution to our conservation costs when normal sources of help had been exhausted. Ultimately, however, it has been the encouragement of the public which has determined the future of the excavations. In the six years up to December 1975 over 300,000 people from all walks of life came to see the site, and the revenue from admission fees and sales of literature made up 95 per cent of the budget. I am deeply grateful to all these people for their help.

Full acknowledgments to all those who have helped directly in this project must await the research reports, but a few should be mentioned here. The greater part of the workforce was provided by senior pupils from northern schools, with the support of their education authorities, and I am particularly grateful to the Northumberland and Gateshead Authorities for their enlightened assistance. Latterly much of the burden has been borne by Task Force Rangers under the auspices of the Manpower Services Commission scheme, and however much one must regret the circumstances which have denied work to so many able young people, one must be equally grateful to the government for supplying funds to provide alternative opportunities.

I owe much to the Vindolanda Trustees and to the Committee of Management, who have endured many long meetings as they sought to solve the problems thrown up by the excavations: their names will be found in the appendix. More than forty scholars have worked on the finds from the site, and I warmly thank all of them. If I single out a few, it is only because I am conscious that the burden upon them has been particularly heavy. Mr Richard Wright and Dr David Thomas of Durham University and Dr Alan Bowman of Manchester University have shouldered the brunt of the work on the writing tablets; Dr John Peter Wild of Manchester University has dealt with the textiles; Dr Mark Seaward of Bradford University has acted as co-ordinator for the bulk of the environmental evidence; Mr George Hodgson of Duncan of Jordonstone College of Art, Dundee, has somehow found the time and the space to deal with the voluminous animal remains; Dr Bob Longmore of Manchester University conserved a daunting quantity of leather and wood; and Mr James Jackman of Booth International Leather Tanners Ltd provided technical help of the highest order with the leather. Mr Les Turnbull, formerly of Heathfield Senior High School, Gateshead, undertook the construction of the replica turf wall, with the ready assistance of his education authority. Professors Eric Birley, Anthony Birley and Barri Jones have supported the work from its inception, as has Dr John Mann; in more recent years I have also profited from the encouragement of Professors Barry Cunliffe and John Wilkes, and Mr George Jobey. Finally, I must pay tribute to my excavators and to my small staff – the former for their cheerfulness and ability to work long hours in uncomfortable surroundings, the latter, Mrs Patricia Birley and Miss Louise Hird, for their undivided loyalty to Vindolanda, in all weathers.

Faults no doubt remain with this book, for which I readily accept responsibility, but there would have been many more without the meticulous and perceptive efforts of the staff of Thames and Hudson Ltd.

I The northern frontier

The historical background

Although the Romans invaded Britain in AD 43, and swiftly established control over the southern region of the island, they made no move to penetrate the north for twenty-five years. They established frontiers on a line between the Mersey and the Humber and against what is now Wales, with substantially lateral roads defended by small fortresses at convenient intervals, and were content to support the native rulers of the tribes beyond the frontiers. Their policy, however, rested upon the maintenance of stable government in Brigantia, the sprawling confederacy north of the Midland plain ruled by Queen Cartimandua and her consort, Venutius, and once the situation deteriorated here, immediate action had to be taken.

The prospect of a northern advance cannot have been attractive. The people were known to be warlike and difficult to control, and they lived in a predominantly hilly and forested region ideally suited to guerrilla warfare. Conquest of these barbarians might bring some economic advantages – the Brigantes were noted for their breeding of good war horses,[1] and the existence of minerals might have been known – but only a complete conquest would allow the gradual withdrawal of the large and expensive army. As events were to prove, this was never possible.

Whatever the long-term Roman plans may have been, their hands were forced in AD 69, when Cartimandua's authority effectively collapsed and put the safety of the Roman province in jeopardy. The governor of Britain, Petillius Cerealis, was ordered to take control of the northern highlands. He carried out the task in brilliant fashion, shattering the army of the rebel Venutius in a series of encounters, culminating in the capture of Stanwick, the huge Brigantian fortress near modern Scotch Corner.[2] Tacitus implies that the Roman forces were withdrawn after the campaigns,[3] but a number of fort sites in the north appear to date to this period. The Ninth Legion was certainly moved forward from Lincoln to a new base at York, and supporting forts may have been placed at Brough and Malton. The earliest Roman remains at Carlisle might be contemporaneous.[4] At any rate, from AD 70 the Roman army was familiar with the geography of the northern region, and even if it did not occupy the area in any strength, we may be sure that there was an effective system of patrols.

Fig. 1

Permanent occupation was not far distant. In AD 79, after half a season in North Wales, Agricola began his attempt to complete the conquest of northern Britain. He knew operational conditions in this country perhaps better than any previous or subsequent governor, having served in the province twice before, initially as a young military tribune on the staff of Suetonius Paulinus and then as general of the Twentieth Legion. In six campaigns, recorded unfortunately only in vague detail by his son-in-law Tacitus,[5] he advanced the Roman frontier to the gates of the Scottish Highlands. Northern England was occupied with the minimum of difficulty, and a frontier was established north of the Forth–Clyde isthmus, with a legionary fortress at Inchtuthil, north of Perth, as the focal point.

Fig. 26

The first timber fort at Vindolanda probably dates from this Agricolan period, when a good road, the Stanegate, was constructed nearby, linking Carlisle and Corbridge, the towns on the two major through-routes into Scotland. Although Agricola failed to complete the conquest of Scotland, and his successors were denied the opportunity by repeated troop withdrawals, the frontier nevertheless remained north of the present English/Scottish border until very nearly the end of the first century. Between AD 95 and 100 changes were made: the major base at Newstead (near modern Melrose) was abandoned – some claim after a disaster[6] – and additional forts were constructed along the line of the Stanegate road, which now became Rome's northern frontier in Britain.

The Stanegate was to remain the frontier for some twenty-five years, and in this period Vindolanda's garrison must have been quite hard-pressed as it sought to protect the road and maintain effective patrols both to the north and south. Roman forts were then still timber-built, and we might expect at least one major reconstruction during those twenty-five years – perhaps more, if enemy action, implied by Roman historians in the early days of Hadrian's reign, had any success.[7] We have no literary sources for the early years of the second century, beyond the mention in Hadrian's biography that he visited Britain and ordered the construction of a Wall, 'eighty miles long, to separate the Romans from the barbarians'.[8] He is believed to have come to this country in AD 122, but some scholars think that his Wall was already under construction by then.[9] Archaeology and epigraphy have given us much knowledge about the Wall in the past century, and we can now give satisfactory answers to many of the questions that perplexed eighteenth-century antiquarians: we know approximately when and why it was built, who the builders were and much of the detail of their building methods. But the intriguing question why the barrier took the form it did remains open to debate.

Hadrian had succeeded his cousin Trajan as emperor in August 117. It was a difficult time. Trajan's wars had seen large annexations of territory to an empire that was already dangerously over-extended, and the treasury was exhausted. Rome needed a man of statesmanship and organizing genius rather than another soldier, yet the emperor's power rested upon the ultimate authority of the armies, accustomed to an almost unbroken succession of victories and triumphs. Hadrian had the courage to call a halt to further territorial advances, and he spent the first years of his reign reorganizing the frontier lines in the western provinces.[10] A permanent physical barrier across the narrow Tyne–Solway isthmus was his ambitious solution to the British conflict, but its size seems out of all proportion to the scale of the problem, far more massive than anything attempted on the Continent.

Hadrian's Wall was built between AD 120 and 130 by craftsmen drawn from the legions stationed in Britain, assisted by auxiliary troops. For the changes in plan and the details of the component parts, the reader must refer to Eric Birley's *Research on Hadrian's Wall* (Kendal 1961) or to the relevant chapters in a general history of Roman Britain (such as S. S. Frere's *Britannia*, London 1967). As a broad outline, however, it can be stated that the new frontier was made up of a number of advance forts to the north of the physical barrier, controlling the old network of roads leading deep into Scotland; a broad ditch fronting the barrier; the curtain Wall (constructed initially of turf in the western sector and stone elsewhere, and of varying width and presumably height); small turrets attached to the Wall at $\frac{1}{3}$-mile intervals between milecastles; a series of forts at roughly $6\frac{1}{2}$-mile intervals along the line of the Wall or very close to it (which were added as an afterthought and therefore displaced some already constructed turrets and milecastles); a supply road linking all the forts and milecastles; a massive flat-bottomed ditch, with small ramparts on each berm, to the south of this road, varying considerably in its distance from the Wall; and, farther south still, the old Stanegate road running from Carlisle to Corbridge, together with its own forts and those along the roads leading south to the legionary fortresses at Chester and York. In addition, in the west at any rate, the Wall system of turrets, milecastles and even forts was continued down the coast, possibly as far as St Bees Head, 40 Roman miles from Bowness on Solway. Professor Barri Jones has recently identified traces of a continuous ditch system in part of this sector.[11]

Those men who had served on the old Stanegate frontier must have been amazed at the new system, which involved colossal government expenditure and a considerable increase in the size of the garrison to about 11,000 troops. The old wooden forts were abandoned: at Vindolanda the main timbers were removed and the site was left to nature as the regiment, possibly the First Cohort of Tungrians, moved forward to the new stone-built base at Housesteads on the Wall, 2 miles or so to the north.[12]

Plate 1; *fig. 1*

Plates 2, 3

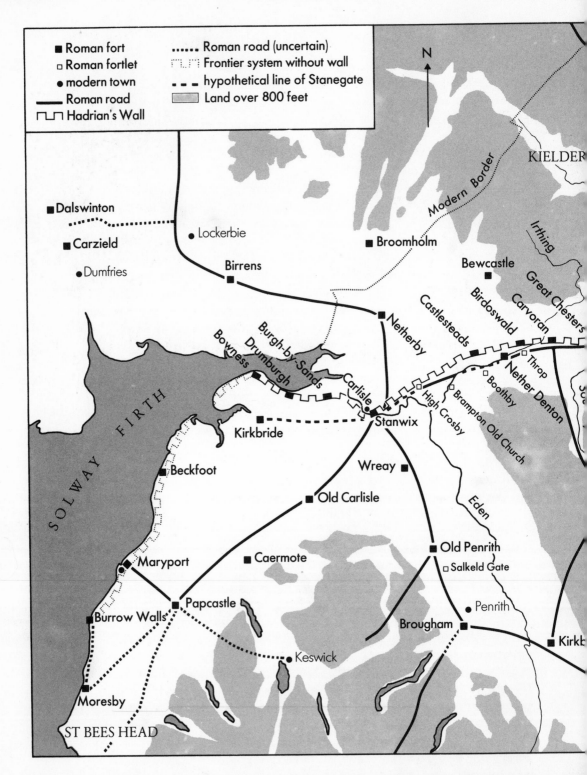

Legend

- ■ Roman fort
- □ Roman fortlet
- ● modern town
- — Roman road
- ⊓⊔ Hadrian's Wall
- ⋯⋯ Roman road (uncertain)
- ⊓⊔ Frontier system without wall
- – – hypothetical line of Stanegate
- ▨ Land over 800 feet

N

KIELDER

■ Dalswinton

● Lockerbie

■ Broomholm

■ Carzield

● Dumfries

■ Birrens

Modern Border

Bewcastle ■

Irthing

Netherby ■

Castlesteads

Birdoswald

Carvoran

Great Chesters

Bowness

Burgh-by-Sands

Drumburgh

Carlisle ●

Throp

Nether Denton

High Crosby

Brampton Old Church

Boothby

Kirkbride ■

Stanwix ■

SOLWAY FIRTH

Wreay ■

Eden

Beckfoot ■

Old Carlisle ■

Old Penrith ■

□ Salkeld Gate

Caermote ■

Penrith ●

Maryport ■

Brougham ■

Burrow Walls ■

Papcastle ■

Kirkb

Keswick ●

Moresby ■

ST BEES HEAD

1 *Map of northern England in Roman times, together with modern place names. The original frontier, the Stanegate, runs just south of Hadrian's Wall, which was built as a more permanent barrier in the AD 120s. The principal Roman roads into Scotland pass through modern Carlisle, Newcastle and just east of Hexham, thus avoiding the moorland and bogs of the central region, now dominated by Kielder Forest*

14

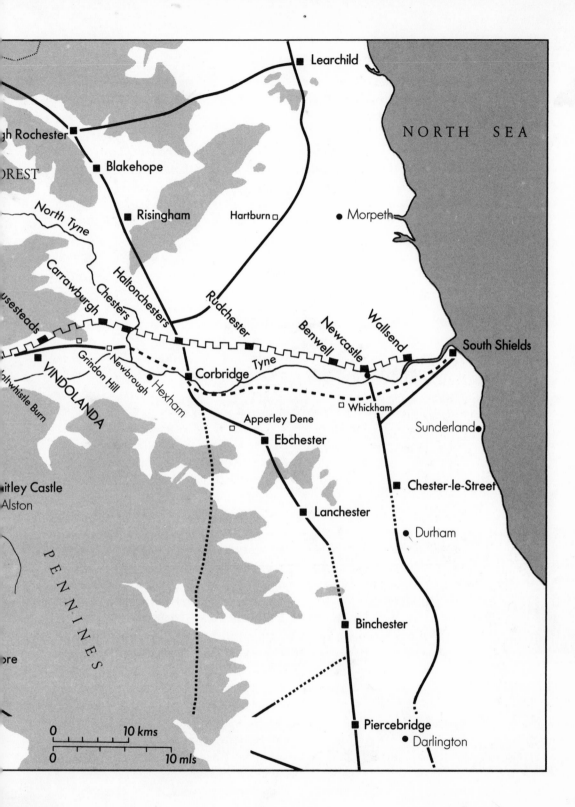

NORTH SEA

Learchild

gh Rochester

Blakehope

ᴏREST

North Tyne

Risingham

Hartburn

Morpeth

Carrawburgh

Haltonchesters

Chesters

Rudchester

Benwell

Newcastle

Wallsend

usesteads

South Shields

Newbrough

Grindon Hill

Corbridge

Tyne

VINDOLANDA

Hexham

altwhistle Burn

Whickham

Apperley Dene

Sunderland

Ebchester

itley Castle

Alston

Chester-le-Street

Lanchester

Durham

P E N N I N E S

ore

Binchester

0   10 kms

0   10 mls

Piercebridge

Darlington

As the frontier garrison planned its routine from its new quarters in the early 130s, the older soldiers must have wondered whether all this activity had been necessary. Forty-five years earlier, Agricola had swept through the region and driven more than 200 miles farther north before annihilating the native army at the battle of Mons Graupius. Yet Hadrian's army, almost as strong and both well equipped and trained, had dug itself into what must have felt like defensive lines, watching out over the deserted moors and forests of Northumberland and Cumbria. Those forces stationed near the great north-south highways – the forerunners of the modern M6, A68 and A1 – might have expected to see a good many natives to the north of the Wall, but in the central sector, from Birdoswald fort to Chesters fort on the North Tyne, there can have been little but wild game to disturb the peace, and Roman commanders must have known only too well that no army could cross what is now the sprawling mass of Kielder forest.

What, then, was the purpose of the Wall? The natives would have been impressed, if not overawed, by this mighty show of engineering skill and administrative efficiency which had occupied its builders for some ten years. The frontier had driven a wedge virtually impossible to penetrate between the sullen inhabitants of the hills south of the Tyne and their brethren to the north, thus removing an anxiety which the troops on the old Stanegate line must always have feared. Henceforth those to the south knew that they were within the empire: those to the north could only enter with permission. In fact the Wall provided a first-class customs and police barrier, and the trade across the frontier, of which we know little but can legitimately speculate that there was much in the way of animal products at least, could be taxed at will. From the military viewpoint the Wall provided a secure base, where men could carry out their training and go about the ordinary business of an army without hindrance, and it gave excellent cover to any preparations for a campaign in the north. But the frontier was never designed as a fighting platform, and it would be wrong to accept the Kipling picture of an army on the defensive.[13] The fighting ground lay well to the north, and the forward forts, with their garrisons of scouts, provided an intelligence service for the commanders on the Wall.

As is sometimes the fate of expensive military projects, the Wall of Hadrian was abandoned less than ten years after its completion, when a new emperor, Antoninus Pius, for a reason which we cannot with confidence explain, ordered the army forward into Scotland once more and built a refined and cheaper version of the Hadrianic frontier between the Forth and Clyde.[14] A caretaker garrison may have remained in the forts on the southern Wall to protect the valuable building materials from looting, but the Tyne and Irthing valleys, the scene of such hectic activity for over twenty years, were suddenly depleted of their huge military, and probably civilian, population. The renewed fervour for an occupation of Scotland did not last long, however, and although the facts and precise dates still elude us, before many years had passed the older Wall had been re-commissioned – perhaps as early as AD 160, perhaps not for another twenty years. Henceforth, apart from a brief spell in the latter part of Severus' reign (between AD 208 and 211), Hadrian's Wall remained the north-western frontier of the Roman empire.

The return from Scotland saw the re-occupation of Vindolanda, which now took its place between Housesteads and Great Chesters as one of the forts *per lineam valli*, on the line of the frontier. Why an additional fort should have been commissioned in what ought to have been the quietest sector of the frontier is not clear. The position of the fort, on the Stanegate road, was a good one, and the prime function of its garrison may have been to protect the heavy traffic between the last fort on the road to the west, at Carvoran, and the river crossing near Chesters, although one would have thought that such a task was not beyond the capabilities of the men already stationed at Great Chesters, Housesteads and Carrawburgh. It is possible that Vindolanda, like Corbridge farther east, served some special function connected with military supplies, and it is hoped that future work inside the stone-built fort will supply the answer to this question. The local area was rich in iron, lead, coal and other natural resources, and the civilian dedication by the *vicani Vindolandesses* to the god Vulcan,[15] patron of metal-workers, may be significant.

After Severus' campaigns in Scotland (AD 208–11), his son Caracalla pulled the troops back to the old frontier, where, so far as we know, they enjoyed a long period of comparative peace. The civilian settlements outside the fort walls grew in size and prosperity, and the frontier district as a whole began to develop its economic potential. The official bar against the marriage of troops was withdrawn – not that there had been any real restriction of unofficial unions before – and son followed father into the regiment that had become identified with its permanent home. Vindolanda might be occupied by a so-called regiment of Gauls, Housesteads by Tungrians, Chesters by Asturians and Burgh-by-Sands by Moors, but it is most unlikely that any of the men had ever seen their regiment's country of origin. For long periods, the only man of continental birth in a regiment might be the commanding officer, a young equestrian undergoing his spell of duty in the armed forces before proceeding further in the civil administration.

We know so little about the history of the north in the third and fourth centuries that we can only generalize from archaeological data. Some claim there is evidence for the decay and neglect, if not actual abandonment, of certain Wall forts in the last quarter of the third century (at Birdoswald,

Plates 4–6, I

Fig. 2

Haltonchesters, Rudchester and Wallsend),[16] and Constantius Chlorus seems to have ordered rebuilding early in the fourth century. But the old frontier of Hadrian was becoming obsolete, although the Roman government never felt confident enough to abandon it altogether. The economy and civil life of the prosperous south was now more likely to be endangered by the gradual corruption of the administration and raging inflation than by invaders from the north or elsewhere, and before long the army in Britain had become as involved in politics as its colleagues on the Continent. Moreover, natives from beyond the frontiers who wanted to raid or trade with Roman Britain now approached by sea rather than the gates of the Wall of Hadrian. Soon Rome developed mobile and heavily armed cavalry units to deal with this new threat, drawing off from possible frontier duty the more ambitious and determined of army recruits. On the south coast, the fleet (Classis Britannica) abandoned its purely military transport role and began to undertake preventive patrolling, supported by a series of great new forts on the south coast at Richborough, Lympne, Portchester and elsewhere. But the Wall frontier continued to function in some fashion, with reduced manpower and efficiency, and after the fright which the southern cities received in the so-called barbarian conspiracy of AD 367, when large parts of Britain were temporarily overrun by Picts, Scots and Attacotti acting in collusion, the Wall was even re-patched and reinforced by Count Theodosius.

By the last quarter of the fourth century, however, the original builders would scarcely have recognized their old forts. The uniform layout had disappeared, and in its place a welter of untidy and irregular structures sprawled everywhere within the fort walls: headquarters buildings and granaries had become living quarters, while bath-houses had long ceased to function. Some men and their families remained in occupation for years or even generations, long after the Roman administration had ceased to function, and it is likely that certain sites, such as Newcastle upon Tyne and Carlisle, were never abandoned. But the Roman army had disappeared. Perhaps even a contemporary could not have said when the end had come.

The modern evidence

In spite of natural decay and the persistent raiding of Roman remains for building materials (begun by the early Christian builders of Hexham Abbey and Bede's monastery at Jarrow), much can still be seen of the old frontier, and a great deal more could be seen if archaeologists had the will and the finance to undertake the necessary excavations. Sad fragments alone remain in the eastern and western sectors, especially at the old sea-port of South Shields or at Benwell on the outskirts of Newcastle upon

Tyne, looking faintly ridiculous amongst massive Victorian red-brick schools or modern housing estates; but in the central sector, in the lovely, wild countryside of western Northumberland and eastern Cumbria, the visitor can still recapture most vividly the spirit of the Roman occupation.

At Corbridge, on the north bank of the Tyne, Roman *Corstopitum* was once the second largest town near the frontier (Carlisle was twice its size), and a small part of the 30-acre site has been consolidated for permanent display after excavation. It is not an easy site for the visitor to understand, for walls of different periods stand side by side, and the town was heavily looted for its building materials (King John also set his army to work here in the hope of finding treasure), but the twin legionary compounds, the massive granaries and the remains of the fine fountain remind us that this was one of the wealthiest sites in the north. Corbridge, however, like Vindolanda, had a long and chequered history, extending back some forty years before the Wall was built, and the visible buildings obscure the traces of many earlier forts constructed largely of wood. A few miles west of Corbridge the remains of all the old frontier components are visible in varying states of preservation, with long stretches of the curtain wall, some turrets and milecastles on display. Both the Wall ditch and the Vallum still drive through the moorland, obstacles now only to huntsmen and tractors. Few visitors appreciate the labour that went into their construction, infinitely the most tedious and back-breaking of all the construction tasks.

At seven of the frontier forts there is sufficient to see to gain an impression, however sketchy, of the old garrison bases. At Chesters, by Chollerford and the bridge across the river North Tyne, the foundations of the great gateways, the headquarters building, a part of the commanding officer's residence and barracks, and the military bath-house are on view at perhaps the pleasantest site of all, but only in aerial photographs can the wide extent of the civilian settlement be observed. At Carrawburgh, the most wind-swept and unattractive of the sites on a dull stretch of moorland, the clay rampart backing stands high, concealing the loss of the stone walls to road builders; but the Mithraic temple outside the south-western corner of the fort has been preserved and displayed after excavation near the overgrown site of Coventina's Well, whose excavation in the nineteenth century contributed so much to the popular appeal of the Wall, with its vast store of over 13,000 coins (there may have been many more, for local inhabitants conducted their own search one evening) and numerous altars.[17]

The heights of the Whin Sill crags were occupied by forts at Housesteads, Great Chesters (more-or-less mid-way between the two terminal forts at Bowness on Solway and Wallsend) and Carvoran, with Vindolanda set back a mile to the south of the Wall between Housesteads

Plates 2, 3

Plate 2

Plate 3

and Great Chesters. Housesteads probably became the new home for Vindolanda's pre-Wall garrison when it was built in the mid-120s, and it presents the best picture now of what a Roman fort once looked like, although its unusually uncomfortable site, on the southern slope of the Whin Sill, created problems for both builders and garrison. It was excavated by R. C. Bosanquet in 1898–9, and by others more recently,[18] and fort walls, interval towers, gateways, headquarters building, commanding officer's residence, hospital, granaries and some barracks were found which are all now on display, together with a fine toilet block; but little can be seen of the once-substantial civilian settlement to the south and east of the fort walls. Great Chesters, partially excavated in the nineteenth and early twentieth centuries, has been allowed to decay with little consolidation of the exposed masonry, although two of its gateways are very fine.[19] Carvoran was levelled by its owner in 1837,[20] but its position on the edge of the Whin Sill crags, high above the Tilpalt burn, is magnificent. Like Vindolanda, Carvoran was an old Stanegate fort, re-commissioned and rebuilt when the Wall was constructed, and it was notable at one time as the home of a regiment of Syrian Archers, the only unit of this type on the frontier. Close to Carvoran, to the east, the glory of the old frontier and the ravages of modern civilization are vividly illustrated by the fine remains of the Wall on the crags alongside the gaping holes created by modern quarries.

Farther west, across the river Irthing and on Cumbrian soil, lies the fort of Birdoswald with perhaps the best preserved of all gateways and the promise, below the turf, of substantial surviving structures.[21] Hereafter, westwards, there is little to see of the forts, which are today largely buried beneath modern towns and villages.

If the Wall forts remind us most forcefully of the Roman frontier garrison, there is much else still visible to show us the magnitude of the building operations and the complexities of garrison service. At several points, but most noticeably at Haltwhistle Burn, traces of the temporary work camps and marching camps can be seen,[22] and at both Chesters on the North Tyne and Willowford on the Irthing there are substantial remains of two of the great bridges which once carried the Wall across fast-flowing rivers. Signal stations, turrets and milecastles are much in evidence, and one milestone, on the Stanegate road below the fort at Vindolanda, survives to its full height in its original position, although cattle have long since erased the inscription. On foot and from the air, the surviving traces of the frontier are considerable: a wealth of material lies awaiting the scholar, who is better equipped than ever before to extract the greatest possible information from the soil.

II   Frontier research and Vindolanda

In 1970 an archaeological trust was set up to organize the excavation and conservation of the site of Vindolanda. This was an event of major potential significance for the archaeology and history of northern Britain. Virtually the whole of a frontier fort and its civilian settlement was now owned by an archaeological charity and was therefore available for extensive research.[23] There were no limitations of time for the work, nor were there restrictions upon its scope. In order to measure the importance of these conditions, we must consider briefly the general state of frontier research, before moving on to a discussion of the site itself.

The state of frontier research

There is no justification for large-scale excavation unless answers are required to specific questions. The purpose of the work at Vindolanda is to illuminate aspects of frontier history which are either little understood or confusing. Research of the past fifty years has already revolutionized our knowledge, but the resulting history is uneven because of restrictions of access to extant sites and the biased choice of sites to excavate made by archaeologists. Developments in the science of archaeology (notably in the field of environmental evidence) have meant that a fresh approach might improve our knowledge substantially. Although it is impossible here to describe in detail the current state of frontier studies (for which readers should refer to the works listed in the bibliography), some major themes must be discussed if we are to see the research at Vindolanda in its proper perspective.

The early history of the frontier is still almost completely unknown. There is a strong suspicion that Agricola's extraordinarily rapid advance through northern England in AD 79–80 must have been made possible by substantially more work by previous governors than Tacitus implies, and we might expect to find pre-Agricolan remains at key places.[24] Carlisle and Corbridge are the two most likely sites for forts established under either Cerealis or his successor Frontinus (predecessors of Agricola), but it is conceivable that Vindolanda might fall into this category as well. The difficulty of dating remains accurately enough to detect a difference of only a few years in foundation is considerable without the chance find of an inscription. But the real challenge is still to gain some detailed knowledge of the north of England's first experience of a Roman frontier, dating from the closing years of the first century, when the armies were withdrawn from Scotland and the Stanegate road became the effective frontier.[25] We particularly need to know how many forts there were on the road, whether the system extended from Corbridge eastwards on the south bank of the Tyne (as seems likely), [26] and whether there is any evidence to point to troubled times, particularly just before the Wall was built.

The intensive activity in the region during the third decade of the second century, as the legions were brought up from their comfortable fortresses farther south to construct the new frontier, is still only inferred rather than proved. Details on the construction of the curtain wall,[27] ditch, turrets, milecastles, forts and Vallum[28] have been examined successfully in part, but the wider problems concerning the nature of the temporary work camps, the location of the quarries and mines, or the role of the auxiliary troops, have been almost entirely neglected, although much information is still there to be found. The examination of the Hadrianic structures is made more difficult by the numerous subsequent reconstructions and alterations, some of them drastic.

Many crucial aspects of the later-second-century occupation are still the subject of intense academic debate. The major questions are those of the motives for the abandonment of Hadrian's Wall *c.* AD 140, only ten years or so after it had been completed, and the return to Scotland with the construction of a new Wall between Forth and Clyde. Was there a military or economic motive for this move? Did it imply that Hadrian's frontier was inefficient, or was it too successful? At any rate, the advance into Scotland heralds the period of greatest difficulty for archaeologists and historians alike, for although there are definitely two phases of occupation on the Antonine Wall – and some see traces of a third here and there[29] – they are exceptionally difficult to date and relate to the subsequent reoccupation of Hadrian's Wall. We know for certain that Hadrian's Wall was once more the frontier of Roman Britain by the second decade of the third century, after the death of the emperor Severus, [30] but it would be a bold author who could with confidence write a history of the period AD 140–212 without a formidable host of footnotes and qualifications.

For the later history of the frontier, we are mainly concerned with tracing the gradual run-down of the occupying forces, which should involve examining barrack buildings rather than the impressive administrative blocks or commanding officers' residences, since the barracks more accurately reflected the strength of the garrisons. Here we should find signs of a decline in standards, of empty buildings, of unusual equipment and so on. Only at Housesteads have such structures been examined in recent years,[31] and the state of their preservation left much to be desired. The work on the Chesters[32] and Great Chesters[33] barracks occurred so long ago that little of significance was discovered (or reported), and more recent excavations at Rudchester[34] and Wallsend[35] have yet to be published in detail.

But if something approaching a history of the frontier is ever to be written, we must obtain information from the civilian and native sites as well as these military establishments; to date our knowledge is little better than a military history, devoid of serious economic and social content. Dr Peter Salway gathered together the civilian evidence some years ago, and emphasized in striking fashion both the quantity of the remains and the paucity of the information extracted from them.[36] Similarly, the efforts of former antiquaries and Ordnance Survey officers, backed up by aerial photography, have demonstrated how many native sites there were in the region – far more than research-workers such as Mr George Jobey and his small band of followers can hope to examine in the near future.[37] But important information is beginning to accrue from these little farmsteads, emphasizing their links with the frontier garrison and their role in the economy of the region.

These then are some of the current problems in frontier research. Their resolution depends to a large extent upon the availability of sites suitable for study. There were at one time seventeen forts on the line of Hadrian's Wall and many more lay within a day or two's march, but until the formation of the Vindolanda Trust none were readily available for unlimited research.[38] Several were buried beneath modern towns and villages: Wallsend, Newcastle upon Tyne, Benwell, Stanwix (the largest fort and the headquarters of the Wall command), Burgh-by-Sands and Bowness on Solway could only be sampled when rebuilding or redevelopment was in progress. Others had modern farm-buildings occupying part of the site (Great Chesters, Birdoswald, Castlesteads and Drumburgh), or were themselves situated on prime agricultural land (Rudchester, Halton-chesters, Chesters, Carrawburgh, Housesteads (civilian settlement) and Carvoran).[39] In addition, even if many of these sites had been available for total excavation, poor preservation or destructive earlier excavations would have prevented all but a few from yielding substantial relevant information. At Housesteads, for example, the whin rock lies close to the surface so that little of the original Hadrianic building survives in the fort, whilst the civilian settlement is scattered over the neighbouring slopes. The proximity of Chesters to the nearby mansion effectively rules out, in the short term, what might be an excellent site, although the extent of the excavations by John Clayton in the nineteenth century may have removed too much of post-Hadrianic material.[40] Carrawburgh, Haltonchesters and Rudchester are all free of modern buildings, but the men who constructed the military road (B6318) over 200 years ago are known to have made good use of the stone in the forts for their building operations, and the road runs through the heart of the latter two forts.[41]

The foundation of the Vindolanda Trust in 1970 was therefore of the utmost importance, for it meant that here at last was a site where it would be possible to examine an entire civilian settlement or *vicus*, forts of the third and fourth centuries, and limited areas of the underlying pre-Hadrianic occupation. Such research would, it was hoped, help resolve some of the outstanding issues in frontier studies.

The antiquarians and Vindolanda

The local inhabitants must always have known of the existence of the Roman remains at Vindolanda, but they were first recorded as such by William Camden in his *Britannia* (1586). It was an intrepid visitor who travelled in these parts north of the Tyne before the eighteenth century, for the border reivers had many strongholds nearby, and three groups of the notorious Armstrong family effectively controlled the region between Housesteads and Vindolanda, using Causeway Farm, Grandy's Knowe and Housesteads Farm as bases for far-flung business operations. Their departure for America in the early years of the eighteenth century, and the industrial expansion of the region, created a safer atmosphere for antiquarians.

A few travellers did reach Vindolanda, and the site gradually became better known through their tireless energy and acute powers of observation. From the pen of Christopher Hunter (1675–1757) in 1702[42] to that of John Hodgson (1779–1845) in 1811,[43] we have a series of accounts by intelligent men of what was then visible and what had happened in recent years – accounts which are all the more valuable because they were written in an age which saw the widespread destruction of Roman remains. The enclosure movement has borne the brunt of academic condemnation, but only because the evidence of agricultural stone-robbing is still so obvious in the field walls, farm-houses and outbuildings which give the present landscape such a distinctive appearance. The late eighteenth and early nineteenth centuries, however, were also years of industrial revolution, and the neighbourhood of Vindolanda swarmed with men bent on winning their living from precious minerals – coal, iron and lead – or stone and clay. The map shows the multiplicity of workings within 2 miles of the site, when for the only time since the Roman occupation the local region was once more busy and prosperous. Not one of those mines

Fig. 2

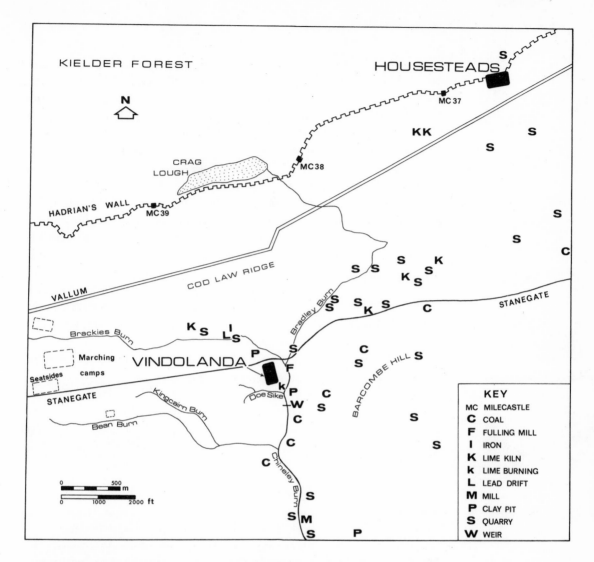

2 The neighbourhood of Vindolanda, showing topographical features and sites of ancient and modern industrial activity. The last of the coal pits closed down twenty-five years ago, and none of the sites is now worked. The period of greatest activity, in modern times, was in the first half of the nineteenth century

and quarries is now worked: the slag-heaps are largely grassed over and the lofty lime kilns are even being scheduled as ancient monuments. The industrial revolution brought with it roads and railways and gave more people access to the free quarries that were once Roman sites. So Vindolanda suffered a twin onslaught from both farmers and industrialists.

Vindolanda is referred to in early histories under a variety of names: Chesters on Caudley, Little Chesters, the Bower and more recently

Chesterholm. 'Chesters' is synonymous for a camp or fortification, and 'Bower' for a wooded copse, which, we understand, was an accurate description of much of the site before the mid-eighteenth century. But the Roman name was undoubtedly *Vindolanda*, as in the Ravenna list[44] – not *Vindolana*, as in the *Notitia*★ – and this is confirmed by an altar and the writing tablets found at the site. It appears to be a Romanized form of Celtic words meaning 'white lawns', a description accurate enough on a summer's morning, when the dew always hangs longest in the field with the Roman remains. Two hundred years ago, seven small crofts stood within 400 yards of the fort walls: one lay just north of the north-west angle of the fort (Smith's Chesters), another stood in the extreme north-west angle of the *vicus* (Wellmeadow Close), a third 100 yards west of this (Archy's Flat), and a fourth nearby (Causeway Farm); two more were situated across the Doe Sike to the south of the *vicus* (High Fogrigg and another un-named), and below the fort, to the east, lay Codley Gate Farm and a fulling mill on the site of what is now Chesterholm Museum. The enclosure movement and landlords bent on improving their property destroyed the crofts, while recent farm amalgamations have left only Causeway Farm as a practising agricultural establishment.

The record of the antiquarians

Plates 7–11, II
Fig. 5

Christopher Hunter described the site of Vindolanda in 1702 and questioned the local crofters. The bath-house, he was able to report, had still been partly roofed a few years before:[45]

> Some years ago ... there was discover'd under a heap of Rubbish a square Room strongly vaulted above, and paved with large square Stones set in Lime; and under this a lower Room [i.e. the hypocaust system], whose Roof was supported by rows of square Pillars of about half a yard high: the upper Room had two niches, like (and perhaps in the nature of) Chimneys on each side of every corner or square, which in all made the number sixteen; the Pavement of this Room, as also its Roof, were tinged black with Smoak.

John Warburton (1682–1759), a shifty excise officer stationed in Northumberland, set some men to work amongst the remains of the site a year or two before 1716 and discovered a fine altar erected by a centurion of the Sixth Legion, Gaius Julius Raeticus, which he promptly removed.[46]

★ The Ravenna Cosmography was compiled in the seventh century A D from earlier sources, and gives details of military and civilian places in the empire. The *Notitia Dignitatum* is a collection of lists of military and civilian staffs whose date and function is variously interpreted by scholars, but which would appear to postdate A D 395 and among which are documents referring perhaps to early-fourth-century British staffs.

The Revd John Horsley (1684–1732), clergyman and schoolmaster, and founder of modern northern frontier studies with his great *Britannia Romana* (London 1732), reported a fine inscription which had been carried across the South Tyne to the little village of Beltingham for re-use as a tombstone.[47] The stone recorded the reconstruction of a fort gateway during the governorship of Claudius Xenophon (223–4), but by Horsley's day all traces of the lettering had been wiped away. Another clergyman and historian, the Revd John Wallis (1714–93), writing in 1765, reported the discovery of what must have been a temple on the western outskirts of the *vicus* – stonemasons had spent many days dismantling its ornate pillars and pilasters – and he also noted the location of one of the cemeteries at Archy's Flat, the small croft a few yards to the west of the present car park.[48]

In 1814 the Revd Anthony Hedley (1777–1835) began his excavation of the east gateway of the fort, and for the first time we can consider that archaeological work, rather than indiscrimate digging, was in progress.[49] Hedley died before he was able to make a report, but, to judge from Hodgson's brief account,[50] the excavation was conducted to a higher standard than most of the nineteenth-century work in the neighbourhood, and was certainly much less destructive than that practised on the Clayton estate at Chesters. Hedley examined the east, north and west gateways of the fort, uncovered stretches of the wall at the north-east angle (sadly, for much soon collapsed), and explored roughly a third of what we can now identify as the commanding officer's residence. Outside the north wall of the residence he found the three great altars which are displayed today in Chesters Museum (the Chesterholm estate was purchased by Clayton in 1864, and most Roman inscribed and sculptured stones were wisely transferred to his own house), and amongst the remains of the west gate about 300 coins from a scattered hoard. In 1831 Hedley moved into the little cottage he had built for himself and called Chesterholm, below the east wall of the fort, the better placed for supervising his excavations. In January 1835, however, when suffering from a heavy cold, he unwisely left his bed to inspect a Roman pot which one of his tenants had located during drainage operations, and his cold developed into fatal pneumonia.

Fig. 19

Fig. 3

Hedley's death closed the first chapter of work at Vindolanda. Viewed from a modern archaeological standpoint, his efforts did not add appreciably to the sum total of knowledge about the site. He had detected at least two periods of construction in the commanding officer's residence, and had demonstrated that the fort's reputation as an excellent source of inscribed stones was untarnished – in the nineteenth century inscriptions were the most important finds. But he had also shown that despite the damage caused by farmers and others, the remains were substantial; the fort wall, for example, still stood to a height of 12 feet at that time.

3 *The finest of the altars (c. AD 222–35) discovered by Anthony Hedley in the commanding officer's house in the stone fort, now to be seen in Chesters Museum. A translation of the inscription reads: 'To Jupiter, best and greatest, and the other immortal gods, and to the Genius of the commanding officer's house, by Quintus Petronius Urbicus, son of Quintus, of the Fabian voting-tribe, prefect of the Fourth Cohort of Gauls . . ., from Brixia in Italy, fulfilled his vow on behalf of himself and his family.'*

Hedley died just before the great age of Wall exploration, the period which saw the gradual transformation of organized treasure-seeking into serious archaeology – the difference between Clayton's early work at Chesters and Bosanquet's comprehensive examination of Housesteads fort in 1898–9. At Chesters, Clayton unearthed fort gateways, a headquarters and fragments of other internal buildings, together with the magnificent bath-house on the bank of the North Tyne, and in so doing he created the interest and uncovered the physical remains which the public took to their hearts.[51] His enthusiasm for the Wall, backed up by the purchase of land on which it lay, saved what was left of the forts at Carrawburgh, Housesteads and Carvoran from further agricultural indignities. It also preserved Vindolanda in anonymity: until 1914, there was no further work there. While Carrawburgh excited everyone with the contents of Coventina's Well,[52] Chesters bath-house showed the full majesty of Wall buildings,[53] and Housesteads[54] and Great Chesters[55] were explored by earnest antiquarians, Vindolanda produced one more altar, as though to remind historians of her former promise. In 1914, during the search for a dried-up well in the western part of the *vicus*, one of Mrs Clayton's workmen unearthed a squat altar,[56] set up in honour of the Divine House and Vulcan by the *vicani Vindolandesses*, the civilians of Vindolanda. It confirmed the reading of the Ravenna list, as opposed to the *Notitia*, that *Vindolanda* rather than *Vindolana* was the name of the site, and it testified to civilian self-government in the *vicus*. It was a major discovery, but the altar appeared too late to take a prominent place in the display at Chesters Museum organized in 1908 by Wallace Budge of the British Museum.

Modern research up to 1970

In 1929 Eric Birley purchased the Chesterholm estate, and Vindolanda returned to the mainstream of archaeological research in a period which saw major excavation along the line of the Wall. His work at Housesteads[57] and other sites limited the amount of time he could devote to the remains on his own doorstep, but he proved the presence of a fort which pre-dated the construction of Hadrian's Wall, confirmed the existence of plentiful civilian remains to the west of the later stone fort, and examined the fine headquarters building. His work will be described more fully in the appropriate chapters. He placed the remains of the fort in the guardianship of what was then the Office of Works in 1939, and the headquarters building, three gateways and stretches of the fort wall were conserved for permanent display. For the first time, therefore, there was something for the general visitor to see.

Figs. 20–23

The outbreak of World War II stopped work at Vindolanda, and after the war Eric Birley's energies were to be fully absorbed by administrative commitments. The pace of excavation in the north had slowed down after the intensive efforts of the 1930s and, although small-scale research was undertaken to answer specific questions, the main task of university archaeologists was that of training their students at summer schools. The Roman site at Corbridge was the best equipped for this purpose and consequently received the most attention.

Vindolanda was now owned by its former tenant farmer, Mr Thomas Harding of Codley Gate, a dour Northumbrian character of the old school whose declared aversions were archaeologists, members of the Department of the Environment and tourists. In 1959 I returned to Vindolanda to examine civilian buildings lying off the south-west corner of the fort in a small field outside Mr Harding's land, and during the six weeks of the excavation he became a regular visitor.[58] These visits laid the foundations for the good relationship between us which subsequently (in 1967) led to his agreement that renewed excavation might be undertaken on his land.

During the summer holidays of 1967–9, I undertook exploratory work in the civilian settlement under the auspices of Durham University Excavation Committee, which confirmed that the *vicus* was well-enough preserved to constitute an ideal site if the opportunity for large-scale work should ever arise.[59] The need for more information about the civilians was pressing, but the nature of the settlements demanded area-stripping, which few farmers would tolerate. My brother, Anthony Birley, and I made several attempts to persuade Mr Harding to sell us the field in which the remains lay, and, although we did not know it until some time afterwards, he was on the point of accepting our offer when he received a better one for the whole farm and sold out.

The formation of the Vindolanda Trust

Thomas Harding sold his farm to Mrs Daphne Archibald, a keen antiquarian, who made her offer in order to prevent the purchase of the property by a farmer hostile to archaeologists. Mrs Archibald then very generously gave the fort field to an archaeological charity, of which my brother and I were among the trustees, and the Vindolanda Trust was born.

Mrs Archibald took possession of the farm in May 1970, and in these circumstances we were able to avoid the necessity of back-filling the important trenches of 1969 (in the *mansio*). In 1970, for the first time, we could operate wherever we pleased in the civilian settlement and put into effect the long-desired area-stripping. But first of all we needed to work out the policy and aims of the Trust.

The main functions of the Trust as eventually agreed and incorporated in the Trust Deeds are given in an appendix at the end of the book. The primary aim it was decided, however, should be the excavation and conservation of the Roman remains. It was soon evident that worthwhile results could not be achieved by limited excavation in holiday periods, and I was able to persuade the trustees that they should attempt to finance full-time research. From 1 April 1971, therefore, my wife and I resigned our respective teaching posts and devoted all our energies to Vindolanda. Gradually we gathered round us a nucleus of permanent staff so that by the summer of 1976, together with a large volunteer contingent, the Trust was employing over 40 people. The fruits of our labours over six seasons are described in the remainder of this book.

III The excavation of the civilian settlement

In 1970 the five-year plan called for a systematic examination of the *vicus* or civilian settlement outside the west wall of the stone fort. Aerial photography and earlier small-scale excavation[60] indicated an extensive built-up area of at least 5 acres, bordered to the north by the Stanegate road and cemeteries, and with the densest concentration of settlement on either side of the two east-west roads leading from the fort and on one side of a road running parallel with the west wall of the fort. An intelligible picture could only be achieved through complete excavation: the work at the Housesteads *vicus* between 1931 and 1934 had shown the limitations of restricting study to building plans at the expense of internal remains.[61] For in a *vicus* Roman orthodoxy and predictability, as seen in the forts, disappears entirely. A rectangular structure of some 60 feet by 20 feet could represent the remains of a temple, a workshop, a domestic house, a stores building or a byre: in other words, the outline plan merely reveals the presence of a building and rarely gives a clue to its function. *Vici*, therefore, demand area-stripping and an open mind.

The optimism of 1970 allowed me to estimate that within ten years we should have as full a picture of a frontier settlement as was possible. I was determined to ignore the temptation of the stone fort nearby: the civilians had been neglected for too long. By 1976, however, little more than a third of the later *vicus* had been examined. In the first place, it was soon discovered that there had been two successive stone-built *vici* of quite different layout, which effectively trebled the amount of time required to examine an area. Secondly, beneath the earlier settlement were located the extraordinary remains of the timber pre-Hadrianic forts (see Chapter VI), which inevitably forced a reappraisal of the excavation programme.

Plates 4, 5

Fig. 4

Fig. 15

Figs. 16, 17

The chronology of the site

Before describing the work in the *vicus*, it is essential to devote a little space to the intricate yet essential matter of dates. In the history of Roman Britain, and especially of its northern frontier, dates are vital – indeed, without them the military historians would have little to argue about. Hadrian's Wall received a formal chronology in the 1920s and 1930s, and its

31

history was henceforth divided into well-ordered components, the 'Wall periods'; in time every excavator fixed the dates of his own site within the accepted framework. In 1970 the skeleton chronology for Vindolanda was that established by Eric Birley and his colleagues on the basis of these Wall periods.[62] It was as follows:

80–125   Flavian or Trajanic fort, perhaps established as early as time of Agricola (80s), but certainly in use from 90 as part of Stanegate frontier

125–163   No trace of occupation in first phase of Hadrian's Wall. (Wall period Ia)

163–197   Construction of a new fort *c*.163 (inscription evidence). Destruction in general disturbance of 196–7. (Wall period Ib)

200–297   Reconstruction of fort in early third century by Fourth Cohort of Gauls. Destruction at end of third century. (Wall period II)

300–367   A new fort constructed early in fourth century. Continuous occupation until 367. (Wall period III)

369–400   Extensive repairs to fort and construction of new buildings after barbarian invasion of 367. Abandonment some time after 400

Initially I adopted this framework and attempted to fit the *vicus* remains into it; the scheme, however, has become increasingly difficult to accept. The fort periods may possibly have differed from those of the *vici*, but this is inherently unlikely, and it is almost certain that the new evidence from the civilian settlement, described below, will necessitate concomitant alterations in the traditional chronology of the fort. In particular it is hard to detect any break in occupation at the end of the second century (where Wall period Ib gives way to period II), and at the end of the third century (where period II is replaced by period III). Instead there appears to have been a gap in occupation sometime in the mid-third century. On the evidence of pottery and coins (and allowing for the inaccuracies of these dating methods), the two *vici* fall within the years *c*. AD 163–350. The gap in occupation, difficult to date precisely, would seem to have been between *c*. AD 245 and *c*. 270 (see below). Thus a new provisional chronology has been followed here, which, for ease of reference, is tabulated in a chronological chart at the end of the book.

As a final word of caution concerning the currently proposed chronology of the site, a recent, and as yet undigested, discovery of coins should be mentioned. At the very end of the 1976 excavation season, a small hoard of 111 coins, terminating in AD 270, was unearthed in one of the last occupation levels of a building from the second *vicus*. Coin hoards can be notoriously unreliable guides to dating, and it is possible for a hoard to be shifted bodily in the course of building operations, but taken with the

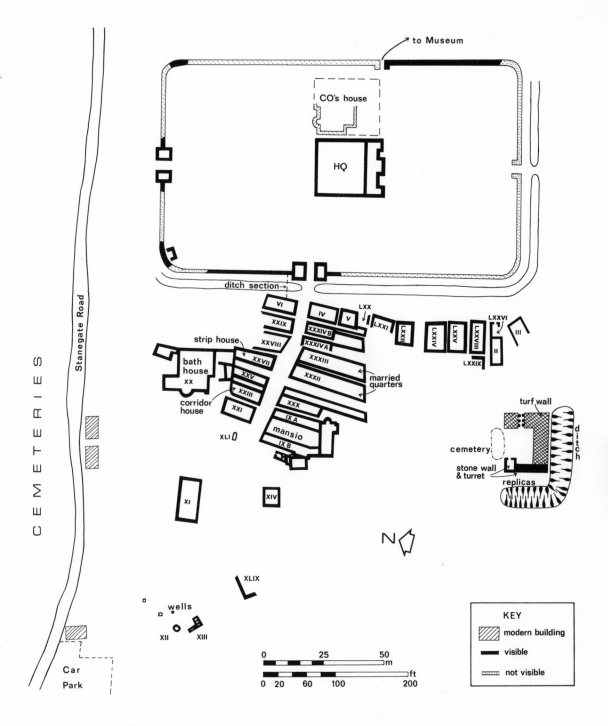

4 Overall site plan of Vindolanda, showing the visible remains. The replicas of Hadrian's Wall lie outside the settlement area, where the plateau begins to dip down into the Doe Sike valley. For separate plans of vicus I and vicus II, see figs. 16 and 17 respectively; for the probable alignments of the pre-Hadrianic wooden forts in relation to the stone fort shown here, see fig. 26; for the stone fort ditch section, see fig. 25. The cemeteries to the north of the Stanegate road have not yet been excavated

paucity of fourth-century coinage in the civilian settlement, it suggests that the dating of *vicus* II to the fourth century may have to be modified in the future.

The initial excavation policy

Plates 4, 5

The choice of the first excavation areas was made for largely non-archaeological reasons. Aerial photography had indicated the extent of the *vicus* remains, but no clear pattern had emerged, partly because of the influence of several small springs upon grass growth, and partly because of the indiscriminate activities of stone-robbers, who had in some cases removed late stone buildings and exposed earlier ones. Moreover, so little excavation had taken place in frontier settlements that guidelines did not exist. If we were to raise the funds necessary for large-scale work, we had also to concentrate upon stone buildings of sufficient intelligibility to encourage visitors to come to see them. The public, however, was so conditioned into thinking of a Roman frontier as being the sole preserve of soldiers that a military building alone would draw them in the first instance. We decided, therefore, to begin with the military bath-house.

The military bath-house

The position of this building was well known, although stone-robbers had concentrated upon it in the past. Military bath-houses had frequently been the objects of archaeological investigation, due partly to their durability, and the general plans of such buildings were not in doubt, although only one example could then be seen on the frontier (at Chesters[63]). But there was the chance that some stratified deposits might have escaped the stone-robbers, and that we might learn more about the detailed workings of the hypocaust system.

Plates 7, 8, II

Fig. 5

Plates 10, 11

In the event, the large changing room and latrine block on the eastern side proved to have been badly robbed, much of the fabric of the building lying spread out amongst the surrounding dry-stone walls. The western portion nevertheless was scarcely damaged, and the walls stood to a height of 7 feet. There was evidence for three periods of construction. At a late date (period 3 on the plan), a rough structure had been built above the old flue to the hot room: the presence of Huntcliffe wares upon its floor suggested that this should be dated to the period after AD 367, when the baths were no longer functioning. Much earlier, the original central block (period 1a), containing the essential bathing rooms and the hypocaust system, had been enlarged in a different style (periods 1b, 1c and 2), with the addition of the changing room and latrine block, the covering-in of the

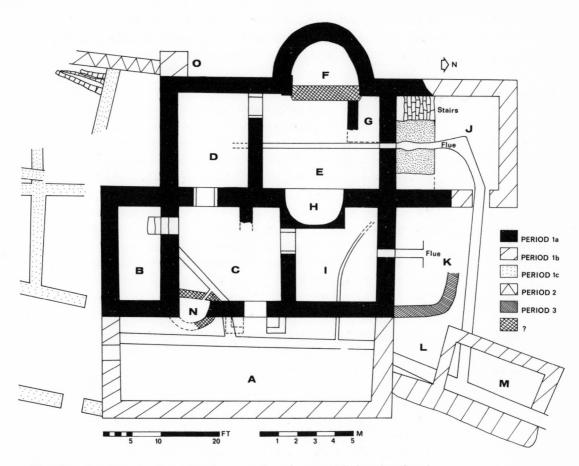

5 *The military bath-house, largely constructed c. AD 160 by craftsmen specially brought in from the Sixth Legion. The changing room (A) and latrine (M) were probably built by the garrison auxiliaries.*

KEY: *A changing room; B cold plunge bath; C lobby; D warm room; E hot, moist room; F hot plunge bath; G hot douche; H uncertain; I hot, dry room; J stoke hole, with boiler platform and steps; K stoke hole; L uncertain; M latrine; N cold douche*

western stoke-hole, and the building of other structures, not necessarily connected with the baths, outside the southern walls. It has been suggested, with reference to other baths exhibiting the same features, that the changing room was a later refinement, but it is difficult to imagine how the baths could have functioned without adequate accommodation for undressing and a decent toilet block. It is perhaps more likely that specialist craftsmen, drawn from the legions, built the difficult central baths block where skill and precision were essential if the flues were to draw properly, leaving the auxiliaries to complete the structure. In this case numerous

Plate 8

Plate 9

bricks, stamped with the legend LEG VIV, were found *in situ* in the hot rooms, and one must infer that the Sixth Legion Victrix (Victorious) had supplied the specialist gang at Vindolanda, as at nearby Carrawburgh and probably elsewhere.

The hot-room floors showed signs of frequent repairs; those in rooms D and E had been refloored at hypocaust level more than once, and two

Plate 11

different types of hypocaust pillars remained – the single-stone shafts and the mortared thin slabs. This stonework was badly perished from the heat and presented considerable problems to the team from the Department of the Environment who had generously undertaken the conservation work

Plate II

for the Trust. The excavation of the warm room (D) proved to be exceptionally unpleasant, for 18 inches of compacted soot remained wedged between the pillars, into which nettles had for many generations thrust their durable roots. The slight chance of finding stratified deposits was further diminished by the discovery of burrows made by rabbits and foxes, who had lived undisturbed in the drains and empty spaces below the floors.

There was no firm dating evidence for the construction of the building. In the make-up of the lobby floor (C) coins found included some of Marcus Aurelius (AD 161–80), Severus (AD 193–211) and Severus Alexander (AD

Plate V

222–35). From the latrine sewer came a homogeneous group of nine bronze *sestertii* ranging from Domitian (AD 81–96) to Marcus Aurelius – in this case, one suspects, someone had dropped his or her purse down the latrine and did not have the courage or the opportunity to retrieve the small change.

The western stoke-hole was well preserved: here a flight of nine stone steps allowed the boilerman to check the level of water in the iron cistern which once stood above the main flue; the lower stones of the arch through which the steam entered the adjoining room have also survived. The whole system was remarkably simple and effective. One powerful fire, perhaps of charcoal fanned artificially, heated the floors of the bathing room, produced hot water for the plunge bath, and generated the steam for the atmosphere. But for the stone-robbing of the early eighteenth century, it would have been possible to light the fires and test the system – after removing the accumulated soot. In the Roman period, boys must have been employed to crawl beneath the suspended concrete floors and clean out the soot.

In these baths the troops relaxed in their off-duty hours, 25 yards outside the fort, and there is evidence from both literary sources and other excavated buildings that here they could have enjoyed delicacies such as oysters and mussels, whilst indulging in various forms of gambling, especially with dice. At such times the soldiers were free from the attentions of their officers, who probably bathed in the suite attached to the commanding officer's residence. But it was evident that others besides soldiers had made use of the building. On the lobby floor and in the main drains which ran out of the cold plunge bath, there were numerous hairpins, beads and delicate box-wood combs, which can hardly have adorned soldiers of the Fourth Cohort of Gauls. Male and female civilians must have been allotted separate times during the day for bathing, for there was no evidence, such as twin changing rooms, to suggest mixed bathing.

The excavation of the bath-house took place in the summers of 1970 and 1971, and it revealed to the public the potential of the site. Building walls stood to a height of 7 feet in places, and the waterlogged drains had produced some exciting finds, notably items of jewellery. The subject of the civilians had been introduced, and the time was ripe for us to turn our attention to the civilian remains proper nearby.

The north side of the main road

South of the bath-house was a series of civilian buildings fronting the main road which ran into the west gate of the fort across a flagged causeway. Excavation of the three most easterly buildings has not been completed, but the others were fully examined in 1971 and 1972.

Sites XXIII, XXIV and XXV proved to be the most interesting of the group. *Fig. 8*
Examination of the latest level of occupation (*vicus* II) suggested the presence of two more-or-less standard 'strip-houses' (sites XXIII and XXV), so called because of their long, thin shape, separated by a 5-foot-wide alleyway (site XXIV) leading through to the baths. Site XXV east of the alley had been heavily robbed, and it was difficult to ascertain whether its room-partitions had been in use in the last phase. One hearth remained in the northern room, set back 2 feet from the western wall. West of the alley site XXIII was better preserved and exhibited an apsidal northern end elsewhere usually reserved for shrines: there was no evidence to explain its use here. Hearths remained in all three rooms, and those in the two northern rooms possessed flues reaching outside the building. There was no trace of industrial activity so the flues may have represented intelligent attempts to improve the draught for the fires.

Either side of the site XXIII and XXV houses were standard strip-houses. The one to the east, site XXVII, possessed a clay-and-stone-built oven in the *Figs. 6, 7* southern room and a raised cooking bench in the northern, a feature which was found to be common in all the last-period dwellings.

The *vicus* II buildings were not large, averaging 60 feet by 15 feet, but they contained three times the space allocated to soldiers' families in the earlier period, and one must envisage them as the homes of family groups

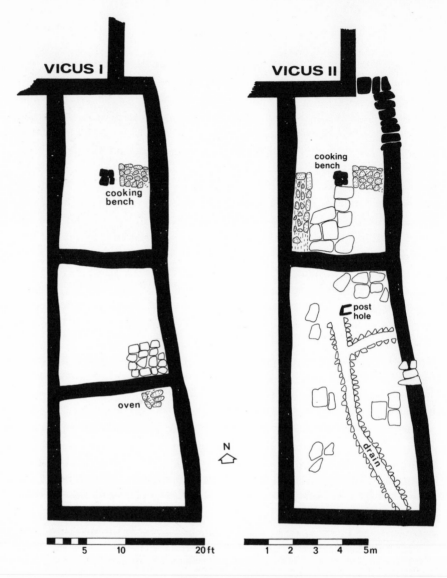

VICUS I

cooking
bench

oven

N

VICUS II

cooking
bench

post
hole

drain

5   10   20 ft

1   2   3   4   5m

SITE XXVII

6 One of the few conventional strip-houses in vicus I, *with typically irregular civilian layout, and its successor of* vicus II, *the only building examined so far that was re-built on exactly the same site*

rather than of single families in the modern sense. It has not been possible to establish whether these houses had a second inhabitable floor, but they must at least have had space among the rafters for the storage of personal possessions and provisions. When in due course attempts are made to calculate the population of the later *vicus* accurately, much will depend

7 *Artist's impression of a reconstructed strip-house. The majority of the civilian buildings were half-timbered, and all appear to have had stone-slated roofs*

upon the estimates for each strip-house: today the average number of people to a house in the north of England is slightly less than three, but 200 years ago it was over six, and in the Roman period it may well have been higher. At an informed guess the population of *vicus* II might have been between about 800 and 1500.

For *vicus* II, therefore, the layout on the north side of the main road was very similar to that found at Housesteads, where a jumble of small rectangular buildings clustered round the roads or tracks leading from the fort, displaying no signs of any attempt at orderly planning.[64] But when the *vicus* II levels were removed a much more intriguing ground-plan became visible. Site XXIII, the alleyway (site XXIV) and site XXV had, it was found, originally formed one large house of a 'corridor' type previously unknown on the frontier. There had been two levels associated with this earlier period, during which the floors had been raised between 4 and 7 inches in height. The debris buried in both floors and fill suggested that the occupants had been distinctly more wealthy than those in the neighbouring houses. In the corridor, below the rubble fill, lay a small gold ring with burnt cornelian gemstones inscribed ANIMA MEA, while a gemstone depicting the god of hunters, Silvanus, was discovered below the doorsill of the south-western room. This latter room possessed several unusual

Fig. 15

Fig. 8

Plate 13
Plate 34

39

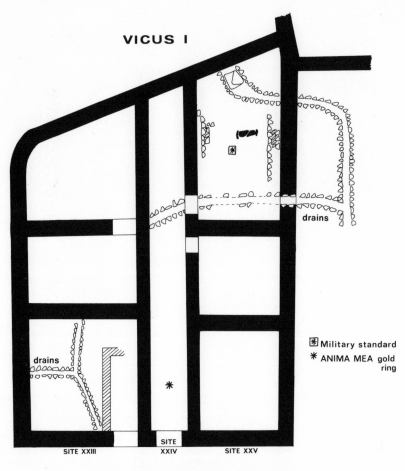

VICUS I

drains

⊞ Military standard
✳ ANIMA MEA gold
ring

drains

SITE XXIII   SITE XXIV   SITE XXV

CORRIDOR HOUSE

Plate 12

Plate 14

features: a narrow wall on the left of the door seems to have been part of a serving counter, and the open triple drains in the floor (which fed into the main roadside sewer) suggest that it was perhaps a butcher's shop, where animals were slaughtered and prepared for sale – the unwanted blood and offal being swilled away into the sewers. The other unusual arrangement was in the northern room of the eastern wing. Here a drain passed through the room, and since it widened out at one point and lacked covering slabs it may have been an internal latrine, the only one from a civilian building at Vindolanda. Buried beneath the earliest floor, in the centre of the room, was the outstanding bronze military standard: how such a revered object came to be hidden below the floor of a civilian building is a complete mystery, for a Roman standard was normally accorded the honour granted to modern regimental colours.

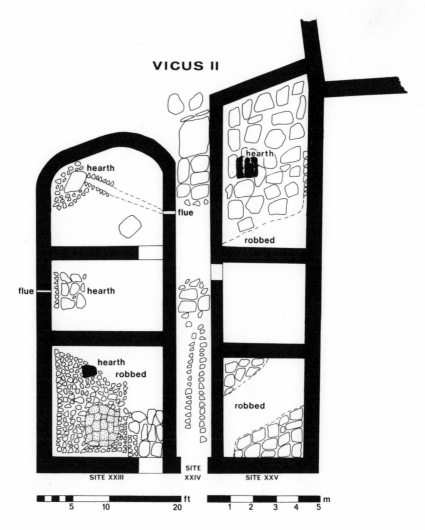

VICUS II

SITE XXIII   SITE XXIV   SITE XXV

8 (Left) *The substantial corridor house from* vicus *I, of a type previously unknown on the frontier, and* (right) *the two dwellings which replaced it in* vicus *II. Findspots are indicated for the military standard and the gold ring, inscribed ANIMA MEA, perhaps meaning 'My Love' or 'My Soul'. The triple drains in the south-western room of the corridor house suggest it may have been a butcher's shop*

Overall, the north side of the main road revealed a *vicus* plan which might have been anticipated, although the corridor house was much more sophisticated than contemporaneous buildings of similar type. The two stone periods on the whole fitted in well with the earlier evidence from the forts; both coins and pottery, however, would have suited a date for the beginning of *vicus* I somewhat before the third century, which is the traditional starting point for the first stone fort. There were numerous coins of Antoninus Pius (AD 138–61) and Marcus Aurelius (AD 161–80), as well as a scatter of earlier issues, but Commodus (AD 180–92) and Severus (AD 193–211) were entirely absent, and the quantity of mid-Antonine Central Gaulish Samian ware much exceeded what could be expected on a site whose foundation did not occur until after AD 200. At this stage in the excavation no attempt was made to examine the underlying levels.

41

The south side of the main road

Fig. 15

In the last phase of occupation (period II), the south side of the main road proved to resemble the Housesteads *vicus* almost exactly.[65] Eight small buildings fronted the road and five more behind them (to the south) faced on to a rough track. Many were damaged by stone robbing (especially those to the west), but cooking benches survived more or less intact in three of them. The majority were obviously domestic houses, although three buildings had been devoted to industrial activity and possessed one or more small bowl furnaces, together with piles of iron slag, while in one room two fragmentary bronze moulds were found. The outstanding feature of all these buildings, however, was their masonry. The builders had dragged huge blocks of freestone to the site, which they had then used for the foundations; some of the blocks weighed $\frac{3}{4}$ ton. Although construction with small ashlar blocks was not entirely unknown at this time, many of the buildings had nothing but these great blocks for their foundations, expertly laid out and lined up, presumably to serve as the base for horizontal timbers and the frame for wattle-and-daub construction. Why the builders should have abandoned orthodox Roman construction is not clear, for they ignored the piles of good masonry lying all over the site and went to the considerable trouble of quarrying fresh materials. At least their new method did not require lime mortar, and this may be the key to the problem.

Plate 15

Having excavated the *vicus* II buildings on the southern side of the main road up to the west gate of the fort, revealing the heavy stone causeway across the fort ditch, we encountered the flagged road which hugged the outer lip of the western ditch and examined the buildings which fronted it. They were very similar to the other period II buildings, although one (site v) was unusual in that it was divided up into several rooms and contained a broad cart door, the stumps of whose timbers remained *in situ*. Three adjacent structures near the south-west angle of the fort (sites LXXIV, LXXV and LXXVIII) had neither cooking benches nor hearths. In the absence of any firm evidence, it seems best to regard them as stores buildings, to house the *annona militaris* or military tribute in kind, which became a feature of fourth-century taxation. Two of them also had large double-doors, through which a waggon could be backed.

Fig. 17
Fig. 16
Figs. 9–11

The removal of many period II structures on the south side of the main road (or probing beneath their floors) revealed a major difference in the planning and function of this part of the *vicus* in the two phases of occupation. The thirteen small buildings of period II had been preceded by only four earlier, period I structures, each very large and quite unlike anything from Housesteads. They have been identified as a *mansio*, or inn for travellers, and three married-quarter blocks. It was later proved that they lay within a massive clay rampart, at least 35 feet thick at base and perhaps originally 12–15 feet high, which probably continued northwards and eastwards (it has yet to be tested) to include the buildings on the north side of the main road. The southern part of the rampart had been examined in 1967 and 1968,[66] when it was mistaken for an earlier military defence, and it is the first example of a defended civilian settlement in the north. How long the defences were maintained cannot be calculated at the moment, although they must fall within the years *c.* AD 163–245, the period of *vicus* I settlement. Nor do we yet know how many buildings lay outside the rampart: there must have been many, for there was no room within for agricultural shacks, forges and temples which every settlement needed.

Fig. 9

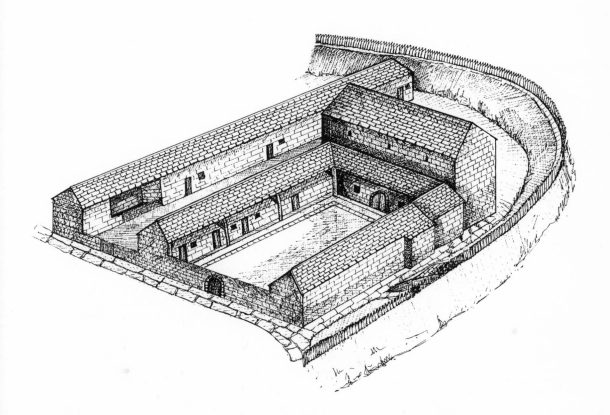

9 Artist's impression of the mansio, *or inn for travellers, after the construction of the clay rampart probably in the late second century. This was the largest building in the settlement, but it did not survive the period of abandonment in the middle of the third century*

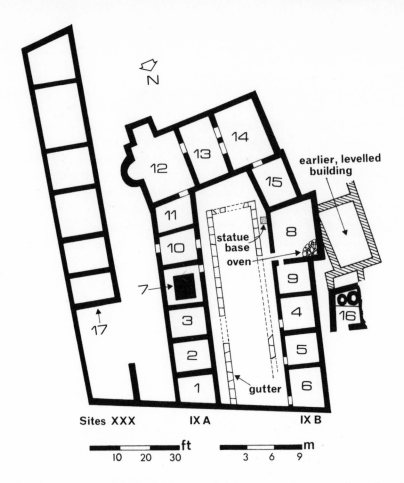

10 The mansio, *or inn for travellers, of vicus I, with the structures to the west – perhaps a brewery, see fig. 11 – built into the clay rampart (not shown). The long, narrow building on the left (site* XXX) *was later separated from the main structure, perhaps becoming another married quarters.*

KEY: *1–6 guest rooms; 7 latrine; 8 kitchen; 9 dining room; 10 stoke hole; 11 baths; 12 baths; 13 entrance loby; 14 ?changing room; 15?; 16 ?brewery; 17 servants' quarters and stables*

The mansio *or inn for travellers*

The *mansio* (site IX) proved to be a complicated building, with signs of much alteration to its layout in the course of period I. The bath-suite (rooms 11–15) contained one furnace and two rooms with concrete (*opus signinum*) floors suspended upon hypocaust pillars, and this was the oldest surviving part of the structure. Work in 1974 showed that the courtyard block, with the six guest rooms, kitchen, dining-room and latrine (rooms 1–9), had been added after an earlier wing had been comprehensively demolished and after the eastern wing, originally the servants' block and stables (site XXX), had been separated and used for a different purpose (probably as another married-quarters block). At some early stage it had

Plate III

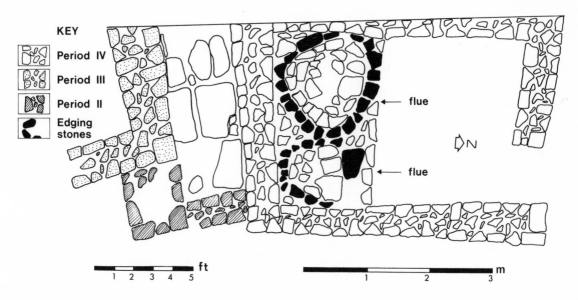

KEY

Period IV

Period III

Period II

Edging stones

flue

flue

ft
1 2 3 4 5

m
1   2   3

11 Structures built into and underlying the clay rampart to the west of the mansio. *The period II and III structures were demolished when the rampart was constructed; period IV, perhaps a small brewery, seems to have been contemporary with the* mansio *in its final years, in the middle of the third century*

been an impressive establishment, sufficiently large to accommodate a dozen officials, together with their servants and baggage animals. But the successive alterations produced an increasingly inferior *mansio*, perhaps because of decreasing use or because its upkeep was too heavy a burden for the *vicani* to bear. In effect, the life of the building reflected the declining importance and the declining standards of the frontier in the later second and third centuries. The bath-suite was the first part to fall into disuse: a structural collapse and the absence of men skilful enough to repair the domed roof of the hot rooms, we may infer, led to the walling up of the doors leading into room 12. The main entrance from the courtyard was first reduced in size and then blocked altogether as room 13 became un-inhabitable, although rooms 11 and 14 continued in use until later. By the fourth century the entire *mansio* had been abandoned.

Plate 16

The servants' block and stables, to the east, were at some stage separated from the main building as we have seen, and this may imply a change of function, perhaps to provide more accommodation for the families of married soldiers. The later constructions of period II *vicus* structures are so massive here that they have been left intact, making the examination of the lower levels impossible for the moment. The small building to the west of

45

Plate 17

the *mansio*, embedded in the clay rampart bank, has two flues below a solid structure containing two circular vats: the flames would have heated the lower stones of the vats. There were few clues as to the building's function, although the number of amphorae fragments was above average. But it was undoubtedly connected with the *mansio* and we have provisionally

Fig. 11

suggested that it might have been a small brewery (the firm evidence for the drinking of Celtic beer was found on one of the writing tablets; see chapter VIII).

A *mansio* at Vindolanda in period I is a reminder that the Stanegate, running past the site, was always the principal east-west trunk road in the Roman period (and for most of the Middle Ages), linking the headquarters of the Wall command at Stanwix with the main legionary armouries at Corbridge. It must always have been a more convenient road than the military way between the Vallum and the Wall, which, although connecting all the forts and milecastles, had to traverse some very difficult countryside, especially on the Whin Sill ridge. Vindolanda was about 24 miles from Stanwix and Carlisle, a good day's march for a Roman traveller, and the next certain accommodation would have been at Corbridge, a further 14 or 15 miles to the east.

We must assume that the principal guests in the *mansio* would have been army officers on the move between posts and civil government officials – census and taxation officers, couriers and the like. But others who could pay would probably have been equally welcome if there was room. Presumably the village council at Vindolanda (see chapter IV) was responsible for the maintenance of the building, although it had clearly been constructed by military craftsmen.

Plates 18, VI

Plates 46, 47

Plates 19, VIII

There was little occupation material in the *mansio* compared with that found in nearby civilian houses or married quarters. The jet betrothal medallion, however, was an important discovery, while the debris covering the remains of the latrine included the fine gold ring, with chalcedony cameo depicting Medusa, and an ornamental belt buckle.

Married quarters

Fig. 12

One of the three substantial buildings identified as married quarters has largely been excavated, with important results. Of the other two, one still lies below the period II remains of sites XXXIVB, XXXV, IV and V, and has only been traced in outline, while the second, site XXX, has such large period II remains above a third of it that no attempt was made to examine the whole building (it was at one stage the *mansio* servants' block: see above). The third (sites XXXII and XXXIII) has been fully examined, except for a small area occupied by a later corn-drying kiln. The western half had been efficiently levelled in the Roman period, but the eastern half was

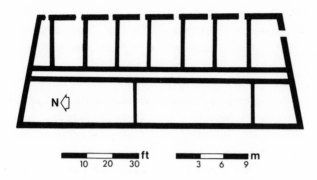

12 Plan of the excavated married-quarters block, sites XXXII *and* XXXIII, *belonging to* vicus *I*

better preserved, with traces of the eight small doorways and three of the partition walls surviving. Although the rooms varied slightly in size, the average dimensions were 12 feet by 16 feet – the same floor space British architects allowed the families of native soldiers in India before World War II.[67] Three of the rooms possessed internal hearths, but cooking was perhaps more often undertaken on the verandah outside. With a floored loft for storage purposes, these quarters were better than a family could expect outside a Roman settlement.

It is logical to assume that the abolition in the early third century of the law which denied marriage to the ordinary soldier should have coincided with government assistance to the resulting wives and children. The provision of orderly accommodation would have been both a sensible and a comparatively cheap way of keeping a measure of control over the development of the garrison *vici*. But a major problem in our acceptance of this argument has been the dating of the married-quarters structures. The pottery from *vicus* I, to which the buildings belong, suggests that they began life some time before the early third century, perhaps as early as AD 163. Pottery evidence, however, is by no means conclusive, since even the greatest experts have difficulty in affirming whether a deposit should be dated to AD 160, 180 or 200 – although most scholars would agree that the Central Gaulish Samian ware found in the married quarters would not have been imported in any great quantity after the civil wars following AD 193. Without an inscription to put the matter beyond doubt, we need to turn to the other possible evidence for dating, the coins.[68] These can be as positively misleading as pottery is vaguely misleading, for coins have a habit of being hoarded and then released, of being counterfeited or dropped down cracks. But the evidence from one important deposit must be considered.

The deposit in question consists of sixty-two coins found in the married-quarters block (sites XXXII and XXXIII), although the majority lay scattered amongst the demolition rubble or in disturbed soil. On the occupation floor of the most northerly room there were seven coins: one each of Faustina I (wife of Antoninus Pius) and Faustina II (wife of Marcus Aurelius) and five of Antoninus Pius. Elsewhere in the building there were sealed coins of Marcus Aurelius (two), Trajan, Hadrian, Sabina (wife of Hadrian) and Antoninus Pius. In other words, the coins dropped during the occupation of the building show a marked preponderance towards the middle and later years of the second century (Antoninus Pius AD 138–61 and Marcus Aurelius AD 161–80); no coins date from later than AD 180. Whilst this might be reasonable for a building occupied *c.* AD 160, it is manifestly unusual for a building which was not constructed until the early third century. One should not make too much of this point, knowing the uncertainties which affected coins and their supply, but similar evidence is suggested by other buildings of *vicus* I (notably the corridor house and the *mansio*).

Another coin deposit from the vicinity of the married quarters has an important bearing on the dating of the two *vici*. The deposit lay in the narrow alleyway or eavesdrip between the *vicus* II buildings (sites XXXII and XXXIII) which were later erected over the remains of the married quarters. There were thirteen coins in this group, ranging from the ubiquitous silver of Mark Antony, through Hadrian and Commodus and up to Tetricus I and II (AD 271–3), Gallienus (two coins) (AD 253–68) and Victorinus (AD 269–71). According to the old Wall-period dating system, the reconstruction should have taken place soon after AD 300, but a date closer to 270 would seem more likely on this evidence. Furthermore, the reconstruction occurred after a period of abandonment – of this there is evidence from many sites in the *vicus* – and whilst we cannot give precise dates to the gap in occupation, the accumulation of earth and the ignorance on the part of the later builders of the previous plans suggests that for some fifteen to twenty-five years (*c.* AD 245–70) Vindolanda was left uninhabited.

The western part of the civilian settlement

Fig. 4

Forty yards to the west of the military bath-house lies a large rectangular building, which was partially examined by Eric Birley in 1930 during his excavation of the pre-Hadrianic ditch nearby. Re-examination of this site (XI on the plan) failed to reveal any trace of a hearth or cooking-bench. The lack of an occupation level, together with the discovery of a single lead sealing, suggests that the building was probably a store. Aerial photography indicates that further stone structures lie west of site XI.

1   View east along Hadrian's Wall from Cuddy's Crag, near Housesteads fort, 2 miles to the north of Vindolanda.

2, 3 Housesteads fort, occupying the most exposed position of any Wall site. (*Above*) Air view from the east; note the traces of the widely spread civilian settlement (*vicus*) to the south and east of the walls. In the foreground, Hadrian's Wall is pierced by the Knag Burn gateway, designed to accommodate civilian traffic. (*Below*) The battered remains of the headquarters building, looking south to the moors beyond the South Tyne.

4–6 Vindolanda from the air, before and after excavation had begun in the civilian settlement. (*Above*) View from the east under a light covering of snow, December 1967, with the Stanegate road on the right; traces of unexcavated civilian structures are visible beneath the turf beyond the fort, as they are in the closer view (*left*), photographed by J. K. St Joseph under drought conditions in 1949. (*Below*) The site from the north in November 1974, after five years of excavation in the civilian settlement (centre right). Chesterholm Museum lies amongst the trees in the middle left margin of the picture and Codley Gate Farm can be seen bottom left.

7   The western wall of the military bath-house, showing the plaster adhering to the outside of the hot-plunge apse.

8   The western wall of the stoke-hole in the military bath-house, showing evidence for rebuilding. (Scale in feet.)

9   Bricks, stamped with the die of the Sixth Legion (LEG[IO] VI V[ICTRIX]), from the hypocausts in the military bath-house. Specialist craftsmen from this legion probably built the difficult central baths block.

10, 11   Interior views of the military bath-house. (*Above*) The ranging pole stands in the principal heating flue. (*Below*) The hot plunge bath, with two different types of hypocaust pillar. (Scales in feet.)

12 The front room of the corridor house (sites XXIII–XXV) of *vicus* I, viewed from the north. The small drains in the floor suggest that this room may have served as a butcher's shop. (Scale in feet.)

13 A gold ring found in the corridor of the corridor house. The cornelian stone in the raised bevel has inscribed on it, anti-clockwise, beginning bottom left, the words ANIMA MEA, which should mean either 'My Love' or perhaps 'My Soul'. The small finger aperture suggests that the ring belonged to a woman.

14   The bronze standard of an unknown auxiliary regiment, found buried beneath the floor of a rear room in the corridor house. The standard would have been mounted on a long pole with forked tripod at the base, and from its side mounts the regimental flag would have hung. How it came to be buried in a civilian house remains a mystery.

15   The heavy stone causeway across the fort ditch, outside the west gate of the fort. (Scale in feet.)

16   The principal entrance to the bath suite of the *mansio* or inn for travellers (*vicus* I, site IX), with two phases of blocking masonry visible. (Scale in feet.)

17   View from the north of the small structure outside the western wall of the *mansio*, interpreted as a brewery. (Scale in feet.)

18　A tiny bronze cockerel found outside the *mansio*, also shown (top left) in colour plate VI.

19　A gold ring (shown also in colour plate VIII) found above the filled-in latrine trenches in the *mansio*. The onyx cameo, badly worn, bears the face of Medusa surrounded by snakes. The small finger aperture indicates that the ring may have belonged to a woman.

20　A small bronze figure, with silver or tin inlaid eyes, found in the western half of the married quarters block (site XXXII). His robe, the *pallium*, suggests he may be meant to represent a sage or scholar.

21 The well (site XII) in the western part of the *vicus*, first examined in 1914. The large, circular well-head once lay behind the stones set on edge. (Scale in feet.)

22 The water-tank (site XLI) on the north side of the main road through the *vicus*, opposite the *mansio*. (Scale in feet.)

23 Settling tanks (site XIII) fed by the well (site XII) $12\frac{1}{2}$ feet to the north-east. Three phases of development are shown. (Scales in feet.)

24 One of the two 'mini-wells' in the western part of the *vicus*, near the settling tanks. (Scale in feet.)

25 Military scabbard chapes found in the *vicus*.

26 Spearheads from the *vicus* intermixed with smaller ballista bolts from the pre-Hadrianic deposits.

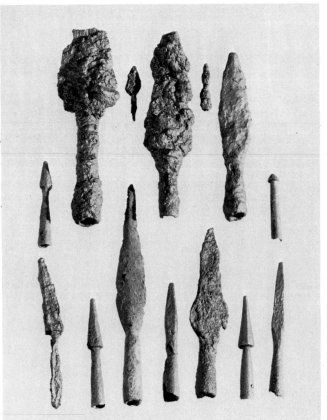

27 A small portable altar found in the civilian store-house (site LXXVIII) outside the western wall of the late fort. The text reads: DIBVS VETERIBVS POS. LONGINVS, which may be translated as 'To the Gods, the Veteres, set up by Longinus'. (See chapter IV.)

28 Another altar, found on the road opposite site V. The text reads: DEO MOGVNTI ET GENIO LOCI LVPVL, which may be translated as 'To the God Moguntis and the Genius of the Place, set up by Lupulus'. (See chapter IV.)

29 An uninscribed altar also found in the civilian store-house (site LXXVIII). The carvings may represent a stylized face or a phallic fertility symbol.

30, 31   Small (headless) pipe-clay statuettes of Venus (*left*) and Dea Nutrix, goddess of fertility and the after-life (*right*). Both figurines were made in a factory at Alliers in Gaul, and were found in the civilian settlement.

32, 33   Two battered reliefs from the civilian settlement representing native Celtic gods. (*Left*) Part of what was once a triad of hooded deities, the mysterious *genii cucullati*, perhaps meant to represent the Veteres, to whom the altar in plate 27 was dedicated. (*Right*) Sandstone relief of Maponus, god of eternal youth, flanked, in niches, by Apollo and Diana.

34–37 Gemstones from the civilian settlement, less than half an inch across, depicting Roman gods: red jasper intaglios of Silvanus (*above left*), Pan (*below left*) and a satyr (*below right*); fractured cornelian intaglio of Jupiter Serapis (*above right*). Cf. colour plate VIII.

38–41 Further gemstones from the civilian settlement: red jasper intaglios of a rural shrine (*above left*) and a maenad (*below right*); cornelian intaglio of Ceres (*above right*); and a bronze bezel from the military bath-house sewers (*below left*) with symbols representing, from left to right, Apollo (sun), Jupiter (thunderbolt) and Diana (moon). Cf. colour plate VIII.

The western part of the *vicus* was notorious for its wetness, and a powerful spring still issued from a Roman well (site XII) which had been examined in 1914 and back-filled after marking with a plaque. On the pretext of helping to drain the land, I had obtained permission from Mr Harding to investigate the area in 1968. It was not possible at first to penetrate lower than 3 feet into the well due to the force of the water, but in the course of laying a pipe-drain we located what turned out to be part of a water-collection system. This was examined more fully in 1973, by which time the spring had dried up. Unfortunately, all precise dating evidence had been removed in the 1914 excavation.

A water-diviner assured me that the well stood above an underground stream which flowed north-south at a depth of approximately 15–20 feet. The masonry of the well had collapsed at a depth of 8 feet and it was judged to be too dangerous to go lower, but cast away near the well was the old well-head, a large circular sandstone basin, from which a fountain had once issued into a series of channels and collecting tanks. One heavy cut-stone channel led away in the direction of the military bath-house, and another, much disturbed by at least four modern pipe-drains, proceeded towards the north side of the main road and the *mansio* collection tank (site XLI). A third fed settling tanks (site XIII) 12½ feet to the south-west, which were originally double tanks with stones set on edge but were later enlarged with masonry. Nearby, to the east, lay two unusual mini-wells, only just large enough to accommodate a bucket and no more than 5 feet deep. They looked like special sockets for large timber uprights, in the manner of goal-post shafts, but in this context they must be associated with water.

However powerful this spring was, it cannot have provided water sufficient for the whole *vicus*. Other wells must await discovery. The site was never short of water, however, for the streams to the east and north of the fort provided a constant supply, albeit somewhat inconvenient to tap, and the little Doe Sike to the south always carried water, except sometimes in mid-summer. One would expect a mill and possibly fulling tanks on the edge of the stream, perhaps near the junction of the burns or by the modern sheep-dip.

In the course of laying the new drains for Mr Harding in 1968, it was discovered that Roman occupation extended up to the field boundary wall on the west, although the material seemed to be largely of second-century date and the structures had been methodically demolished. Somewhere near here, according to the Northumbrian historian Wallis, lay the ornate temple which masons destroyed in the early eighteenth century.[69]

Plate 21

Plate 22

Plate 23

Plate 24

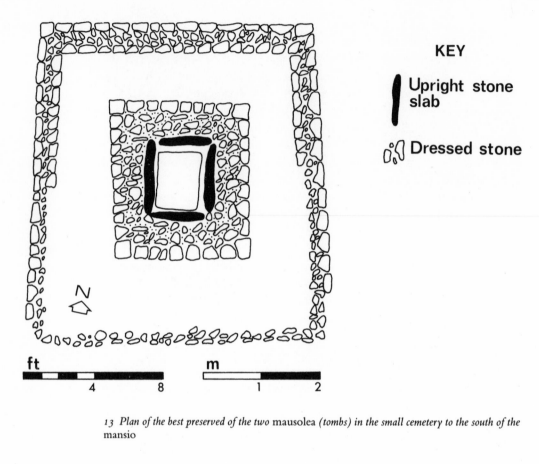

KEY

Upright stone slab

Dressed stone

13 Plan of the best preserved of the two mausolea *(tombs) in the small cemetery to the south of the* mansio

14 Artist's impression of the reconstructed mausoleum

The cemeteries

Although John Hodgson had drawn attention to the possibility of a cemetery 'in a swampy close' to the south-west of the site,[70] the principal burial grounds were known to lie to the north of the Stanegate road, stretching from opposite the north-western corner of the fort for nearly $\frac{1}{2}$ mile westwards. The eighteenth-century tenant of Archy's Flat, mid-way between the present car park and Causeway Farm, frequently disturbed burials in the course of gardening, and aerial photography also showed masonry-built tombs farther east, nearer the fort. These areas lie outside the Trust property in good hay-fields, and there is little prospect of excavation in the foreseeable future. We did, however, locate a small and probably late-fourth-century cemetery to the south of the *mansio*, close to the replica stone turret. Six graves were examined in 1973: two proved to be small *mausolea*, with a burial chamber surrounded by a masonry wall, and the remainder consisted of two lintel graves and two slab graves, all orientated north-south. Boulder clay lay very close to the turf at this point, and the bones had not survived. There were no grave-goods present and, in spite of the north-south orientation, this may have been a small Christian burial ground. In addition, at the extreme western end of the Trust property, two cremation burials pre-dating AD 250 were discovered during the construction of the present car park.

Figs. 13, 14

At some stage during the excavations it will be necessary to examine a large number of burials to complement the information from the structures and artifacts, but for the present we must rely upon the work carried out on the Romano-British cemetery at Trentholme Drive, near York, discussed in the next chapter.

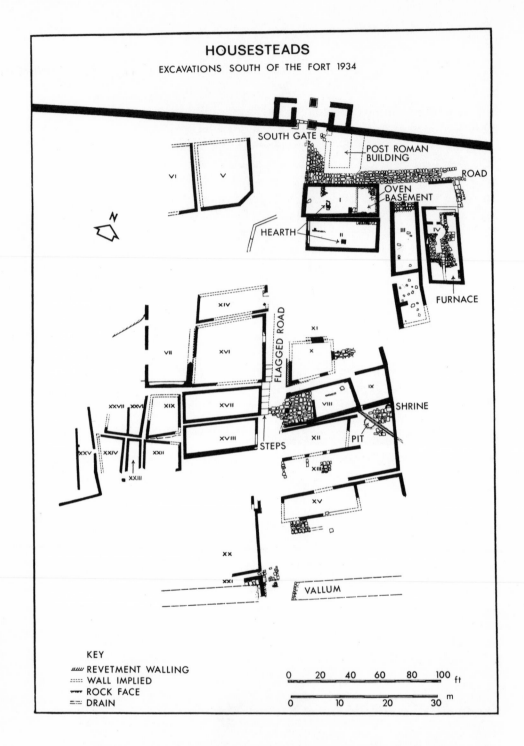

HOUSESTEADS

EXCAVATIONS SOUTH OF THE FORT 1934

SOUTH GATE

POST ROMAN BUILDING

ROAD

OVEN

BASEMENT

HEARTH

FURNACE

N

VI

V

I

II

III

IV

XIV

XI

XVI

VII

X

FLAGGED ROAD

IX

XXVII XXVI

XIX

XVII

VIII

SHRINE

XXV

XXIV

XXII

XVIII

XII

PIT

STEPS

XXIII

XIII

XV

XX

XXI

VALLUM

KEY

〰 REVETMENT WALLING

⋯⋯ WALL IMPLIED

➤➤ ROCK FACE

═ DRAIN

0   20   40   60   80   100 ft

0   10   20   30 m

15 *Plan of part of the civilian settlement at Housesteads, excavated by Eric Birley in the 1930s. The jumble of more-or-less rectangular strip-houses fronting the road leading from the fort bears much closer resemblance to vicus II than vicus I at Vindolanda*

IV   The civilians of Vindolanda

After six years' work on the *vicus* it is worth taking stock to consider how clear a picture we can now portray of the inhabitants of a frontier settlement. In 1970 the civilians were described, when they were mentioned at all, merely as the appendages of the troops, living in often squalid circumstances outside the walls of the frontier forts. The main evidence for this view came from the excavations of the Housesteads *vicus* conducted before World War II. Yet little more than a fifth of this settlement had been examined, and the major effort had been expended on obtaining the external, fourth-century plans of the buildings.

Fig. 15

Although we have done our best to keep an open mind at Vindolanda, inevitably there have been some preconceptions. Housesteads had demonstrated the spread of the ubiquitous strip-house, the more-or-less rectangular building with its short side fronting the street or track. Both Housesteads and Binchester[71] had shown that several of these structures possessed open-fronted rooms leading directly on to the street, typical of many Mediterranean shops even today. But the outstanding buildings were likely to be the military bath-house, official temples and perhaps the *mansio*. On the Hadrianic frontier such extra-mural structures had already been encountered at Benwell (temple to Antenociticus and possibly a *mansio*),[72] Rudchester (Mithraeum),[73] Chesters (bath-house and, through aerial photography, a *mansio*),[74] Carrawburgh (bath-house, Mithraeum and Coventina's shrine),[75] Housesteads (bath-house, temple of Mars and Mithraeum)[76] and Great Chesters (bath-house).[77]

The only literary reference to civilians was a single brief mention by Arrian, recording the presence in the early second century of merchants and veterans in a fort *vicus* at Phasis in Cappadocia.[78] There had been no investigation of a Roman cemetery on the frontier, although epigraphy, from the evidence of tombstones[79] (and allowing for the bias of chance discovery and the wealth of the deceased), had suggested that some civilians at least were rich and sophisticated, and that not all these were members of commanding officers' households. In fact, common sense and analogy with more recent armies of occupation indicated that the influence of the civilian upon the social and economic life of the region must have been immense: civilians were more than just the families of the soldiers.

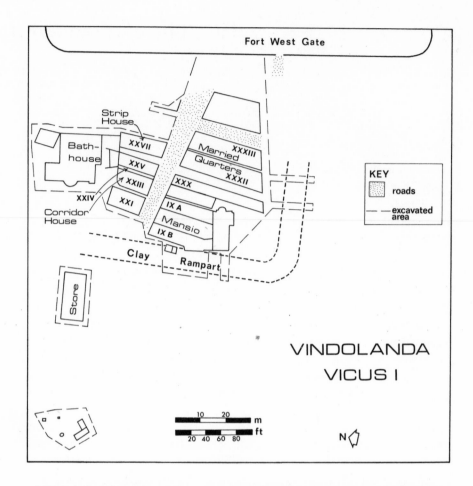

16 Vicus I, the civilian settlement of c. AD 163–245, in relation to its stone fort. The clay rampart may have been added at the close of the second century ; it was levelled before the construction of vicus II, c. AD 270

We hoped, therefore, that a comprehensive examination of a well-preserved frontier settlement would reveal something positive about the role of the civilian. What follows is an account of our findings so far.

The two civilian settlements

Current evidence suggests that the *vici* were contemporary with the stone forts, but that this chronology no longer corresponds with the traditional dating of the Wall periods (see chapter III). *Vicus* I would therefore appear to fall within the years *c.* AD 163–245, and *vicus* II *c.* AD 270–350. The gap in

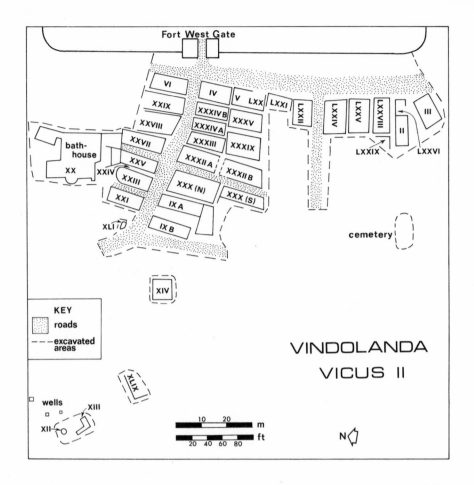

17 Vicus II, *the civilian settlement of* c. AD 270–350, *in relation to its stone fort. It is estimated that nearly half the settlement has been excavated, and that the areas immediately to the east and west of the military bath-house are as densely occupied as those to the south. Few stone buildings lie in the western part of the field, although occupation material extends as far as the wells, sites* XII *and* XIII.

occupation of some 15–25 years (*c.* AD 245–70) is confirmed by the very different styles of the two settlements, indicating that the builders of *vicus* II knew nothing about the detailed plans of *vicus* I. After the upheaval of AD 367 the settlement continued to be occupied in a limited way for many years, but whether it was finally abandoned in AD 400 or AD 500 we cannot as yet determine.

Although less of the first *vicus* has been examined than of the second, we know enough to state that it bears no resemblance to the Housesteads *vicus*, the enclosed area of about 2 acres being much more akin to a military-built annexe within a defence system. The strip-house here is the exception

Fig. 16

rather than the rule: the area so far examined contained only two of these distinctive civilian houses, opposite three large married-quarter blocks and a *mansio*. A military bath-house lay to the north. Roads were of excellent standard, broad and solid, and the principal drains – masonry conduits five courses high, flagged top and bottom – had apparently been laid down before the construction of the buildings. The finds suggest a high standard of living for the 500–800 inhabitants – certainly comparable with that of the soldiers within the fort – with much imported pottery and no industrial activity.[80] Further work outside the defended enclosure may alter this picture, but the contrast with other *vici* is nevertheless marked.

Fig. 17

The period II *vicus*, with a population of roughly 800–1500 occupying an area of 6–10 acres, was much more like that at Housesteads. Thirteen more-or-less conventional strip-houses stood above the remains of the three married-quarter blocks and the *mansio*, and even the corridor house was split into separate dwellings. On the evidence of the plans alone this represents an entirely different style of life, with much less government assistance and organized town-planning than before. Looking beyond the plans, the changes appear even more marked. Industrial activity was much in evidence – notably metalworking, including the manufacture of bronze objects – coinage was scarce (and often consisted of well-worn and early issues), and the superstructure of the buildings was now predominantly of timber. Drainage had become haphazard and inefficient, particularly in the southern parts of the settlement. Pottery was markedly inferior and often of local manufacture. It is curious that there were many more signs of weapons in this later *vicus* – arrowheads, lead sling-bullets, spears – yet there were no defences, and even the western ditch of the stone fort had been allowed to silt up into nothing more than a drainage channel. Perhaps as military efficiency declined it became necessary for civilians to protect themselves.

Plates 25, 26

Vicani Vindolandesses

We still know little about the physical characteristics of the *vici* inhabitants. The few graves examined in 1973 in the small cemetery south of the *mansio* contained only slight traces of burials, and we have no proper skeletal remains. The main cemeteries lie in the field to the north of the Stanegate, outside the Trust's property, and others lie to the west. In the absence of more direct evidence, we must rely upon Mr Peter Wenham's excavations of the Romano-British cemetery at Trentholme Drive, York to give us information about the physical type, diet deficiencies and life expectancy of these people.[81] It is unlikely that the Vindolanda civilians were radically different from these less wealthy inhabitants of Roman York, 100 miles to the south. Civilian frontier tombstones recording age at death provide additional supporting evidence. We should, therefore, be dealing with a very young community, where the average age of death for men was about thirty-six and for women twenty-eight (ignoring infant and child mortality), a picture not unlike that which was normal in England throughout the Middle Ages. There would have been almost no diet deficiencies, and arthritis and rheumatism were probably the most frequent diseases, although outbreaks of plague may have taken an increasing toll towards the end of the fourth century. Many would have been partially crippled by half-healed wounds and fractures, but in general they were sturdy people, of similar height to the modern British. The *vicani Vindolandesses*, although of cosmopolitan stock, were largely bred on the site: they were natives of the area, and would never have thought of themselves as being in any way foreign.

We now possess several of their names. Altars to British gods were set up by Senilis, Longinus, Senaculus and Lupulus, names which would appear to be thinly disguised Roman forms for native appellations.[82] Graffiti on pottery include the names Martinus, Gatinius and Aurelius. But of the thousands of women who must have lived and died at Vindolanda, we know only of Flavia Emerita and another with an equally orthodox Roman name beginning 'Aurelia'. It is evident from the graffiti that literacy declined as time wore on.

Plates 27, 28

Religious beliefs

As portrayed by the inscribed and sculptured statuary, the religion of the civilians was predominantly Celtic. No temples have been located so far, although one period II building did have a small semi-circular shrine built into it (site xxx), and the Revd John Wallis, writing in 1765, recorded the discovery and dismantlement of a temple west of the *vicus*.[83] The village council (see below) set up an altar to the Roman god Vulcan and a relief to Mercury was found re-used in a cooking-bench on site LXXII, but apart from these only the popular pipe-clay statuettes of Venus betray classical influences. Thus the recent work has yielded five dedications to the Veteres, one to Moguntis, one to the Mother Goddesses, one to Maponus (together with a relief of the deity), and reliefs of perhaps Matrona (mother of Maponus), the strange hooded gods (the *genii cucullati*), and a pipe-clay statuette of Dea Nutrix. This latter seems to have come from the Rhine and the Mother Goddesses were popular throughout the Celtic world, but the remainder are all British – primarily northern British – deities. The identity of the Veteres god (or gods) is still in doubt, even though we now have more than fifty dedications concentrated in the central sector of the Wall

Plate 30
Plate 27
Plate 28
Plate 33
Plate 32
Plate 31

between Birdoswald and Chesters. Dedicators invoked the god as a single or multiple, male or female, deity, which suggested to Dr Anne Ross, one of the foremost authorities on Celtic religion, that the Veteres might therefore not be a particular god but the general name used to invoke any one of a number of northern gods, perhaps the equally mysterious *genii cucullati* triads or the Mother Goddesses, both also found at Vindolanda.[84] We have as yet no proof for this theory however. The three other Celtic deities represented at Vindolanda – Moguntis (a god similar to the Veteres), Maponus (god of eternal youth) and Maponus' mother, Matrona (an important deity in her own right) – are also native to northern Britain.

Plates 27, 32

Plate 33

Plate VIII
Plates 35, 40
Plate 34

Plates 36, 37, 41, 39

But if the altars and sculptured stones point strongly to the predominance of Celtic faiths, the evidence from the gemstones and rings is quite the reverse.[85] The Roman pantheon is represented by the Capitoline triad, Jupiter (twice), Juno and Minerva, and by Mars (twice), Mercury (twice), Fortuna and Silvanus. Another stone, with a carving of a stag, is perhaps also associated with Silvanus, whilst the remainder are largely classical portrayals – Pan (twice), a satyr, a maenad, Ceres, agricultural scenes (twice), a bull, Daedalus (perhaps) and two indeterminate male figures. This is a world far removed from Maponus, Moguntis and the Veteres, yet the gemstones are normally thought to indicate the religious sympathies of the owners. Are they, then, the veneer of Romanization, purchased from an enterprising merchant and worn without serious appreciation of their symbolism? Or is it a case of insurance, such as we often find in military dedications (and nowhere more clearly than in the celebrated case of the centurion M. Cocceius Firmus, who made dedications to as many as twelve deities at Auchendavy on the Antonine Wall),[86] where the Roman and native gods are worshipped in the same breath? Whatever the social and religious implications, the gemstones do suggest the existence in northern Britain of a refined craft, whose practitioners could achieve superb results with very difficult and tiny stones.

The terracotta statuettes also imply the dominance of Roman over Celtic faiths. Four of the popular Venus statuettes were found, for example, as opposed to only one relief of Dea Nutrix, the sole Celtic deity represented. Three other fragmentary terracottas cannot be assigned to any particular deity with confidence, although one fine head, from the western ditch of the stone fort, still bears traces of black paint on the face, hinting perhaps at a North African origin, possibly during the reign of the first African emperor, Severus (AD 193–211).

Plate IV

Christianity presumably reached the northern frontier by the middle of the fourth century at the latest. No adequate proof of this, however, has been forthcoming, even though there is some evidence to suggest that the small cemetery located in 1973 was for Christian burials – for the friends, perhaps, of the Christian Brigomaglos, whose tombstone was found many years ago in a field to the north of the site and may date from the end of the fifth century at the earliest.[87]

Animal husbandry and agriculture

Soil conditions over much of the site are in general perfect for the preservation of bone. Two major deposits have been found, well stratified and separated by nearly 200 years in time. That from the western ditch of the stone fort, dating from the closing years of the fourth century, is probably a civilian deposit, thrown into the ditch by the occupiers of the houses nearby; the older deposit is military, lying sealed in the floors of the early wooden forts. Analysis of these bones is supplying vital statistics about the development of animal husbandry in the north during the Roman occupation, together with the relative popularity of different meats.[88] Already we have evidence for the predominance of beef, followed by mutton and pork, but there are also a large number of deer bones (and one of the writing tablets shows that venison was issued from the military stores in the early second century: see chapter VIII), some goat, horse, dog and cat. The dog bones (skulls, shoulder blades and leg bones) were found in association with the butchered beef and mutton, suggesting that dog was sometimes eaten.

Animals played a much more important role in everyday life than they do today. A major part of the population was actively engaged in trades dependent upon them – hunters, farmers, transport-drivers, weavers, butchers, leatherworkers, horners and so on – and the feeding, breeding, slaughtering, salting, storing and selling of meat products took up much time. Milk, lard, meat, eggs and marrow were all important products, whilst virtually all clothing came from the backs of animals. Transport required horses, asses, mules and oxen, and a good proportion of the armed forces also needed horses. But animals provided far more than this. Candles were necessary for artificial light, and bone was employed for knife handles, combs, hair-pins, needles, picks, pegs, spades, dice and gaming-pieces. Besides clothing, leather was used for buckets, bags, hats, harnesses and tents, and hair was woven into ropes strong enough to fire the heavy catapults. The list is endless, without pausing to consider the requirements of sport, religion, and vermin control.

It is at any rate certain that the civilians were not short of meat. As regards grain, it can be assumed that the bulk of the supplies, both for the troops and the civilians, came from the corn-growing areas of the south and were shipped to the Tyne by the Classis Britannica. The Wall region has never been noted for its cereal crops, and it is unlikely that productivity was any higher during the Roman period. Whether cereals were in fact cultivated locally we do not know, since later agricultural activity seems to have destroyed all traces of the Roman field systems close to the site. There are no cultivation terraces nearby of the sort so prominent on the southern slopes of the Housesteads hillside or the moorside near Newbrough, but in any case the lie of the land scarcely suited this practice at Vindolanda. The civilians also collected and ate nuts, especially from the widespread hazel tree, and the local countryside would have been rich with fruit-bearing trees and berries. The cabbage stalk found in the well of the stone fort's headquarters building is the only surviving evidence so far for vegetables, but we may be sure that they were in plentiful supply.

Industry

Fig. 2

Plate 42

Signs of industrial activity are confined to period II. Pottery was imported from outside the region in both *vici*, but in the later period the crude so-called 'Housesteads ware' became increasingly common, as did other wares which are scarcely distinguishable from those found on outlying farmsteads throughout the Roman occupation. There is little doubt that pottery was being manufactured at Vindolanda, perhaps down by Chineley Burn, close to clay pits which were still being exploited 200 years ago. Iron was plentiful in both periods, and was probably mined and smelted locally – indeed, the *vicani* dedication of an altar to the Roman god Vulcan, patron of metalworkers (see below), must be significant. There were good supplies of iron ore on the north bank of Brackies Burn, only 300 yards north of the *vicus*, and a nearby lead drift may also have been worked by the Romans. Coal was definitely mined and used in civilian houses, but not to any large extent, and the plentiful supplies of local timber probably satisfied most needs. Other industries detected in the recent excavations have been bronze-working, weaving and spinning (probably a household chore), lime-burning (for the mortar) and the manufacture of shale objects. Tanning and milling can also be inferred.

Village dwellings

Domestic dwelling houses were plain by the standards of wealthy homes farther south, being devoid of mosaics and wall-plaster (although the latter was found in both the military bath-house and the *mansio* bath-suite). In period I houses were ashlar built, of local sandstone quarried from the crest of Barcombe Hill 500 yards to the east, while in period II they were largely of timber, resting upon solid stone foundations. Roofs were uniformly

covered with stone slates $\frac{3}{4}$ inch thick, pinned on to the rafters with single   *Fig. 7*
iron nails, and windows were usually timber shuttered (although the
corridor-house appears to have had window-glass, as did the bath-house).
The corridor-house and *mansio* of *vicus* I both had internal latrines, as
befitted buildings designed for wealthier civilians, but otherwise there was
little provision for sanitation in either period, and it would be no surprise to
find a communal latrine building somewhere. In strong contrast to a town
like Corbridge, there were no architectural frills and little ornamental
stonework. Two of the period II houses contained traces of wattle and
daub, and the majority possessed stout masonry and raised clay cooking
benches. There was no surviving trace of furniture, and on the analogy of
the early wooden forts, the floors were probably carpeted with bracken and
straw. In contrast to the native dwellings out in the countryside, these were
strong and roomy dwellings, the simple homes of soldiers' families,
craftsmen and peasants.

Household and personal articles

If the civilians lacked the sophistication of the town dwellers, they
nevertheless possessed all the material comforts of Romanization. Their
doors had strong locks, their windows iron bars; wells and water-tanks
provided a good water supply close at hand. They had numerous iron and
bronze utensils, and their feet were well shod – even those of their small
children. The womenfolk decked themselves out in beads, hairpins,   *Plate VI*
bangles and rings, combed their hair with delicate box-combs, plucked
their eyebrows with bronze tweezers and admired themselves in polished
mirrors. Nor did the menfolk deny themselves highly decorated bronze
tunic fittings and belt attachments; some of the enamelled buckles they   *Plate VII*
wore were minor works of art in their own right.

The analysis of the jewellery has been particularly rewarding. Dr Martin
Henig's work has shown that this class of find is now almost as useful as
coins and pottery for dating purposes, and considerably more useful for
giving a pointer to individual dress and wealth.[89] Brooches were used by   *Plate 44*
both men and women to fasten cloaks and tunics; at Vindolanda they range
from early trumpet forms, just coming into use at the end of the first
century, to the rare penannular animal-headed brooch, which may have   *Plate 43*
been the property of a late-fourth-century Theodosian mercenary. Signet
rings were ornamental, religious, but also functional objects, with which
letters were sealed and documents validated. Of other types of jewellery
there are only two earrings (from the commanding officer's residence in
the early wooden forts and from a civilian building near the bath-house)
and one pendant (the jet betrothal medallion from the alleyway east of the   *Plates 46, 47*

77

mansio), but there are numerous beads and hair-pins. The beads are mainly glass, and range from large blue segmented-melon types to the small green-and-blue types, sometimes rectangular, but more often cylindrical or ovoid. Particularly fine are the clear glass beads, laminated with gold leaf, which are usually taken to be late second century in date. The hair-pins, of bone or bronze and strictly functional, have none of the fine decorated heads sometimes found elsewhere.

Conclusion

Plate 45

The civilians, therefore, adopted the dress and the merchandise of their government. They frequented the military bath-house, and must have possessed some leisure if they had time to undergo the normally elaborate ritual there. They bought and sold goods with Roman money, although perhaps only during period I, since there is some indication in period II that coinage was scarce and barter returned. Their language, however, is unknown. It may have been a form of pidgin Latin, or it may have been Celtic: the influence of the army must have determined this, and we cannot be certain what the practice of the later Roman army was. In general, their standard of living was higher than that of any of their successors until the eighteenth century.

We call them civilians, but we must recognize that at all times their lives were inextricably intertwined with those of the soldiers. Military routine, army pay, the sound of the bugle and marching boots must have been as significant to them as to the soldiers in garrison. One wonders, therefore, what happened to the *vicani* when a regiment or strong detachment was posted overseas: no doubt many families managed to accompany the troops, in the manner of later armies, and if the Roman Higher Command valued morale it may have offered official assistance in such cases.

The bond with the army had given birth to the *vici*, so it was natural for the *vici* to disappear when the army departed – if it really did depart. In the past, scholars were able to assert, with some confidence, that the frontier was deserted by AD 383, 388 or 400 (normally on coin evidence[90]), but few still hold to this view. The withdrawal of troops from Britain towards the end of the fourth century affected the new field armies more than the old, neglected and now inefficient frontier forces, and what little evidence there is suggests that men continued to reside in some of the Wall forts for many years, even after AD 410 when the official link with Rome was severed. If they did so, we can be sure that civilians remained as well.

But the closing years of the fourth century certainly witnessed a major decline in the civilian population. The disruption of trade routes, the drying up of the supply of coinage and persistent outbreaks of plague would have had the same devastating effects in the north as they appear to have had in the south; it was the field armies which now attracted ambitious merchants and craftsmen. Local industry must have declined and subsistence farming become the principal source of livelihood. The land alone, however, could not have supported as large a population as was once maintained comfortably at Vindolanda and elsewhere. Very gradually, no doubt, the Vindolanda *vicus* died.

Such, then, are our thoughts on the *vicani* after six years' work. Some important questions have yet to be answered. We still know little, for example, about the government of the settlement, although an inscription found in 1914 seems to provide evidence for a village council ('For the Divine House and the Powers of the Emperors, the villagers of Vindolanda set up this sacred offering to Vulcan . . .'). Together with three other similar inscriptions from the north, it demonstrates that self-government did exist in certain *vici*.[91] But as much remains to be excavated as has been examined so far, and we must hope that the second five-year campaign will provide some of the answers to present problems.

I View of Vindolanda from the west in 1974, with Barcombe Hill beyond and the Stanegate road running down the left-hand side of the picture.

II Hypocaust pillars in the warm room of the military bath-house, with the hot plunge bath beyond (to the north).

III View north over the eastern wing (site IXB) of the *mansio* or inn for travellers, with the latrine (room 7 in *fig. 10*) in the centre of the picture.

I

II

III

V   The stone forts

The two main excavation campaigns

Before the formation of the Vindolanda Trust, excavation in the fort had been confined very largely to two campaigns, separated by 100 years in time and by a gulf of experience. Anthony Hedley's work in the early nineteenth century was never fully published, and all but the inscribed stones which he found have disappeared (although, fortunately, his trenches appear to have been back-filled before stone-robbers could exploit them). It is clear from Hodgson's précis of these excavations that Hedley had located the bath-suite of the commanding officer's residence and identified the presence of more than one period of construction.[92] He explored the east, north and west gateways, finding a scattered hoard of more than 300 coins in the latter, which proved occupation in the middle years of the fourth century. The architecture of these gateways was unimpressive compared with the monumental structures in the forts on the Wall, and a flight of stone steps rather than a road led away from the east gate. Hedley's greatest success was the discovery of the three fine altars lying outside the northern wall of the commanding officer's house, which proved that the Fourth Cohort of Gauls had been in garrison here during the early years of the third century.[93]

Fig. 18
Fig. 19

Fig. 3

Like so many people after him, Hedley had visions of uncovering the complete fort:

> Half-a-dozen labourers for a fortnight, at an expense of not more than five pounds, would clear away much of the rubbish from any one of these stations, and not only discover, it is to be hoped, many curious and precious fragments of antiquity, but throw a very interesting and desirable light on the stationary economy of the Romans, and on the form and arrangement of their *castra stativa*.[94]

This estimate of the men, money and time required for the task was as wide of the mark as Agricola's celebrated calculation for an Irish campaign; today we seem no nearer to Hedley's goal than he himself was 150 years ago.

The second campaign at Vindolanda, conducted by Eric Birley between 1930 and 1936, established a firm sequence for the site. The dimensions of

Plates 48, 49

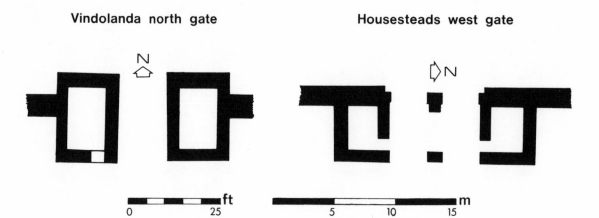

Vindolanda north gate **Housesteads west gate**

18 The architecture of the late stone fort was utilitarian compared with that of the Wall forts, such as Housesteads, built 150 years earlier, and this is particularly evident at the gateways

the uppermost stone fort were proved (508 feet by 306 feet, giving an area of just over $3\frac{1}{2}$ acres),[95] and the evidence for three periods of occupation, with the latest being securely dated by sealed coins to the late fourth century (Wall period IV as it was called), allowed him to bring the later history of Vindolanda into line with the chronology of the frontier recently worked out in collaboration with Gerald Simpson and Ian Richmond. Birley stated the case for the linking of the construction of the period I stone fort to Wall period II (starting soon after AD 200), the new period II fort to Wall period III (starting AD 300), and with major reconstruction and alterations after the chaos of the barbarian conspiracy (AD 367). The two main phases are therefore usually referred to as Severan and Diocletianic, after the emperors of the time, and the third Theodosian, after the count who restored order following the barbarian conspiracy. As we have seen, this dating framework has become increasingly difficult to accept in its entirety in the light of new evidence.

Eric Birley achieved much more than the establishment of a sequence. Inside the fort, he re-excavated the three gates Hedley had examined (and caused them to be preserved for visitors to see), fully explored the fine headquarters building and examined a catapult platform and other features of interest. To the west of the stone fort, he partially explored a *vicus* or civilian-settlement building (site XI), suggesting that it had been a store constructed in the second century, and below it he found traces – ditches and ramparts – of a timber fort which had been built at Vindolanda long before Hadrian came to power, dating from the days when the Stanegate

Fig. 26

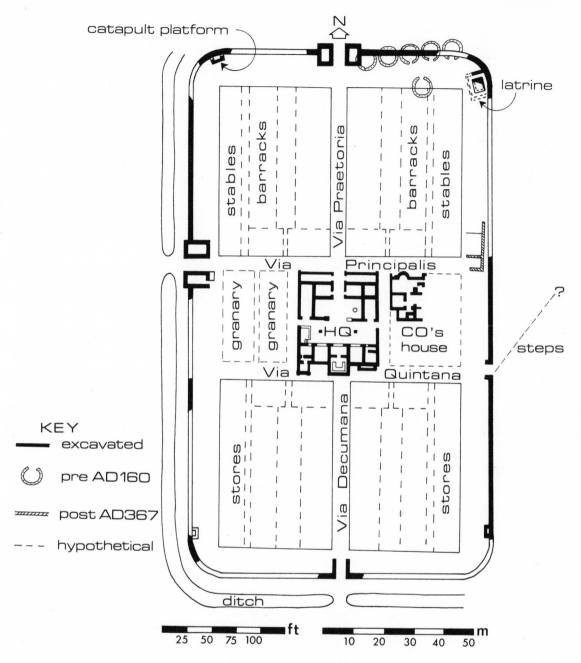

catapult platform

N

latrine

stables
barracks
Via Praetoria
barracks
stables

Via Principalis

granary
granary
·HQ·
CO's house

Via Quintana

?

steps

KEY

—— excavated

◡ pre AD160

▨▨ post AD367

- - - hypothetical

stores
Via Decumana
stores

ditch

ft
25 50 75 100

m
10 20 30 40 50

19 The late stone fort, showing excavated structures and hypothetical outlines of stores, granaries and barracks. The function of the circular structures (fig. 24) to the east of the north gate, which pre-date the building of the fort, is not known. Note the lack of guard chambers at east and south gates road formed the northern frontier of Britain. The pottery lying in these early ditches suggested a Trajanic date (AD 98–117), but Birley felt that the fort might have been founded as early as the Agricolan era (AD 80–5).

The results of research

Fig. 2

Only a limited amount of excavation has taken place inside the stone fort since Eric Birley's work in the 1930s, but as the fort and its garrison is such an integral part of the whole site it is worth studying closely. The fort lies at an altitude of 530–45 feet, occupying the eastern side of a moderately level plateau which overlooks the junction of the Bradley and Brackies Burns (where they become the Chineley Burn and later the Bardon Burn, flowing into the South Tyne 2 miles away). The steep, narrow valley of the Doe Sike is situated immediately to the south. There are long-distance views in the same direction of the wooded Allen valley and the Pennines, but elsewhere the outlook is limited – by Barcombe Hill to the east, Cod Law ridge to the north (obscuring most of the Whin Sill ridge, on which Hadrian's Wall was built), and with a gentle upward incline to the west towards Seatsides giving no more than 2 miles visibility. Vindolanda, however, was never selected as a fort site for its views, but rather because it lay on the Stanegate road and spacing demanded a fort hereabouts in the original scheme. Granted that within a mile or so a fort had to be built, the location chosen was the only one possible. It was reasonably flat (although not as flat then as it is now); there was an excellent water supply (which has preserved so much of the Roman material and yet made the excavations unusually difficult); and the slopes leading down to the streams provided good drainage.

Recent research, to be discussed in the next chapter, has shown that this initial military occupation of the site took place as early as the late first century AD, when the Stanegate was the northern frontier and a wooden fort stood at Vindolanda. As soon as Hadrian's Wall was built, however, the garrisons moved forward to the new frontier, abandoning Vindolanda to nature (*c.* AD 125). It was not until some forty years later that the site was reoccupied and a new, stone fort erected. Henceforth, to judge from the *Notitia* list,[96] it was reckoned as a fort *per lineam valli*, taking its place between Housesteads, 2 miles to the north-east, and Great Chesters, 4 miles to the north-west.

The 1930s' excavations determined conclusively that two stone forts had once stood upon the plateau, and that the later one had been much repaired after AD 367. What today is less certain is the precise dating of the two main phases. Eric Birley's original proposal of early-third- and early-fourth-century dates respectively will have to be revised as a result of the latest work in the *vicus*. There is at least a case now for regarding the first stone fort as being of late Antonine date (after *c.*AD 163), and the second fort as being nearer to AD 270 than AD 300. Further work is necessary before the matter can be settled, but there are important consequences at stake, not the least of which is the composition of the garrison. The Fourth Cohort of Gauls, part-mounted and 500 strong, is known from inscriptions to have been at Vindolanda from the early third century and, depending upon one's views on the dating of the *Notitia*,[97] it may have been there for most of the fourth century as well. Whether or not, however, the regiment was present at Vindolanda as early as AD 163 it is difficult to say. The Fourth Cohort of Gauls was a much-travelled regiment.[98] It had been stationed at Templebrough in Yorkshire before the end of the first century, and later (*c.*AD 125) served at the Wall fort of Castlesteads, west of Vindolanda. After this, it left records of duty at both Castlehill (after *c.*AD 140), on the Antonine Wall between Edinburgh and Glasgow, and at Risingham (*c.*AD 150/60), the outpost fort on Dere Street, 20 miles north of Corbridge. The second century was a period of fluid movement for the auxiliary regiments in the north, and it is just possible, though unlikely, that the Cohort of Gauls did reach Vindolanda as early as 163. If the original garrison was not this cohort, it will be interesting to learn one day who did build and occupy the unusually fine stone fort in the late second century.

Aerial photography, which revealed so many of the buried structures in the *vicus*, tells us little about the fort, since there is such a deep spread of rubble masonry that the building walls remain hidden. For information about the fort we can rely only upon the excavation reports and the conserved masonry.

The headquarters building

The largest, most ornate and important building in any fort was the headquarters (*principia*). The example now visible at Vindolanda is substantially that of the period II stone fort, since the post-AD 367 modifications have been almost entirely removed in the course of excavation and conservation.[99] The building faced north towards the Stanegate road and proved to be a more practical and compact building than others of its type on the Wall. The military architecture of the later third and fourth centuries was less elaborate than it had been in Hadrian's day. There were no draughty colonnaded courtyards at Vindolanda: an open-ended verandah (13 and 14 on the plan) faced the main road (*via principalis*), but the courtyard (12) was little more than a token affair, being surrounded by rooms housing the armouries (*armamentaria*, 8–11). The large cross-hall (7), once impressively roofed, contained a well-preserved

Figs. 21, 23
Plate IX

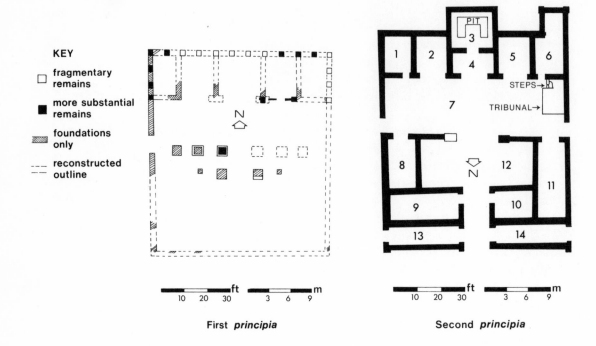

KEY

☐ fragmentary remains

■ more substantial remains

▨ foundations only

--- reconstructed outline

First *principia*

Second *principia*

tribunal or commanding officer's rostrum at the western end. The administrative rooms were approached from this hall: the two end rooms (1 and 6) by 3-foot doorways, but the inner three (2, 4 and 5) by impressive broad entrances, originally arched over. The entrances to rooms 2 and 5 had been reduced in width by fine ornamental stone screens, carved with rectangular patterns. In between these rooms lay the *aedes* (4), the chapel where the regimental standards were once displayed, and behind it, projecting south 10 feet, lay a sunken pit for the pay and savings (3), protected both by double-width walls and the sanctity of the regimental chapel. The two eastern rooms (1 and 2) were the offices of the regimental standard-bearers, who dealt with matters such as pay and savings, hence the worn tops of the ornamental screens in their outer office and the holes for an iron grille. An additional room had been built on the rear of these offices at some stage – perhaps in fact during the main alterations after AD 367 – and it proved to be a neat little latrine. The western pair of rooms (5 and 6), occupied by the regimental adjutant (*cornicularius*) and his staff of clerks, also had an extension to the south, a small heated inner office.

There were drastic alterations to the whole building after AD 367 (stone period III). All the *armamentaria* received ventilation channels beneath their floors, as if they now acted as stores for more perishable commodities, and a well, 20 feet deep and dug down to bed-rock, was inserted into the small

Plate 50

Fig. 22

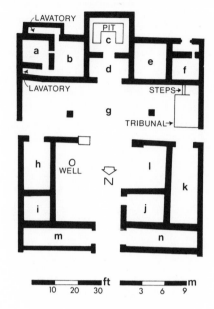

Third (Theodosian) *principia*

20 (Opposite left) The southward-facing early headquarters building (principia) of the third century, examined by Eric Birley and Ian Richmond in the 1930s. This unusual structure could only be fully excavated if the later building (fig. 21) were removed

21 (Opposite right) The second, northward-facing headquarters building of the fourth century, substantially that now on display.

KEY: *1, 2 standard-bearers' offices; 3 strongroom; 4 chapel; 5 adjutant's office; 6 clerks' office; 7 cross-hall; 8–11 armouries; 12 courtyard; 13, 14 verandah*

22 (Left) The third, northward-facing headquarters building, dating from after AD 367.

KEY: *a–f living quarters; g cross-hall; h–k stores; l courtyard; m, n stores*

23 (Below) Artist's impression of the late stone fort's headquarters building before the alterations made after AD 367

courtyard. The excavation of the well revealed a fine collection of Roman wood (samples of oak, birch, willow, hazel, ash, yew and pine) and leather, together with the skulls of ten oxen and a cabbage stalk.[100] The broad cross-hall was retained, but now pillars were needed to support its roof. The administrative rooms became living quarters, with their own hypocaust system, and perhaps functioned as the quarters of the new commanding officer, although examination of the old residence will be necessary before we can be certain. In the ante–chapel of the *aedes*, a fire had

Plate 48

burned for many years, emphasizing as forcibly as anything else that the new regime had broken with the strict traditions of the past.

Fig. 20

The *principia* of the periods II and III stone forts stand above the remains of their period I predecessor, a most unusual and ornate structure which was effectively demolished by the rebuilders. The outline of its plan was recovered in the 1930s, but it was never fully excavated. It looked south, not north, and some of its walls had been faced with a relief embodying the Sun God in his chariot, together with small statues once attached to a background. Sadly, the interpretation of these fragments was interrupted by World War II, and when the time came to re-examine them prior to publication it was discovered that they had disappeared from the storeroom of Housesteads Museum. One fragment alone remains, an angry clenched fist. The building had been constructed using the *adobe* method familiar in Roman Spain and Africa. 'The softer material . . . is cut up into panels and divided by piers of hard stone. Further, not trusting the softer material even then to carry the required weight, the builders laid only a few courses of ashlar, and set upon the sill, so formed, panels of soft sandstone ground to powder and mixed with tile and lime, so as to form a hard lime concrete.'[101] One wonders why Vindolanda should have received such an unusual headquarters building, quite unlike any other built in Britain.

The commanding officer's house

Fig. 3

Hedley's work in the commanding officer's residence is known only from the brief description left to us by his friend Hodgson, but it seems to have been a complicated and spacious building, and much reconstructed. Outside its northern wall Hedley found the three fine altars which now grace the display in Chesters Museum, set up by prefects of the Fourth Cohort of Gauls – dedicated to the Genius of the commanding officer's house by Pituanius Secundus, to Jupiter and the other immortal gods and to the Genius of the commanding officer's house by Quintus Petronius Urbicus, and to Jupiter and the Genius and Guardian gods by another commanding officer whose name does not fully survive.[102] On the Wall, at both Housesteads and Chesters, one can gain an impression of the spaciousness of these houses, which were designed to provide worthy accommodation for men of good birth who applied their skills to the military profession for perhaps only a few years before returning to civilian government service or to private life as landowners, etc. Their homes in the forts were large enough to cope with a household – wife, children, servants and slaves – and it is thought that their bath-suites probably catered for the regimental officers as well. Quintus Petronius Urbicus recorded on his altar the fact that he was the son of Quintus, of the Fabian voting tribe, of Brixia in Italy, and he was one of the few men of Italian birth to serve on the northern frontier. The majority of commanding officers were of provincial origin.

No barrack buildings or stables have been examined so far, and only when they have been excavated will we have any idea of the actual strength of the Fourth Cohort of Gauls, part-mounted. Their paper strength was 500, and judging by evidence from documents elsewhere this figure was only an approximate guide. We do know, however, that there were the orthodox granaries to the west of the headquarters building, for a trench cut across the area in the 1930s proved the point, although it was evident that these structures had been converted to accommodation in the last phase of occupation.[103] There is also certainly sufficient space inside the fort for the traditional eight barrack buildings – six for the infantry centuries and two for the four *turmae* of the cavalry – together with two stables and two general stores.

The circular structures

The excavators in the 1930s examined very carefully the area to the east of the north gate, seeking stratified evidence to date the structures.[104] As is so often the case, they created more problems than they solved, for below the rampart mound, and disappearing beneath the foundations of the fort wall, they found a series of circular structures with internal diameters of 14 feet, 2-foot-thick walls, good 3-foot doorways, and no trace of hearths or ovens. These structures preceded the fort wall, but below them there was a patch of flagging above a drain, and below that, sealed by clean clay, lay the sleeper trenches of a pre-Hadrianic structure. Neither the date nor the function of these buildings are known. One cynical academic suggested that they might be a Roman model village, designed to set the natives an example,[105] but others, more practical, felt that they might be mills for grinding the regimental corn ration. Whatever they were, and whatever their date of construction, it will take a great deal more excavation to fit them into any scheme of periods.

Plate 49

Fig. 24

The catapult platform

Inside the north-west angle of the fort, there was a large catapult platform. Filled solid with rubble and clay, its side walls were not bonded in with the fort walls, giving the structure sufficient elasticity to survive the recoil. A machine mounted at this point would have controlled the difficult approach to the northern gate of the fort. It would be reasonable to expect

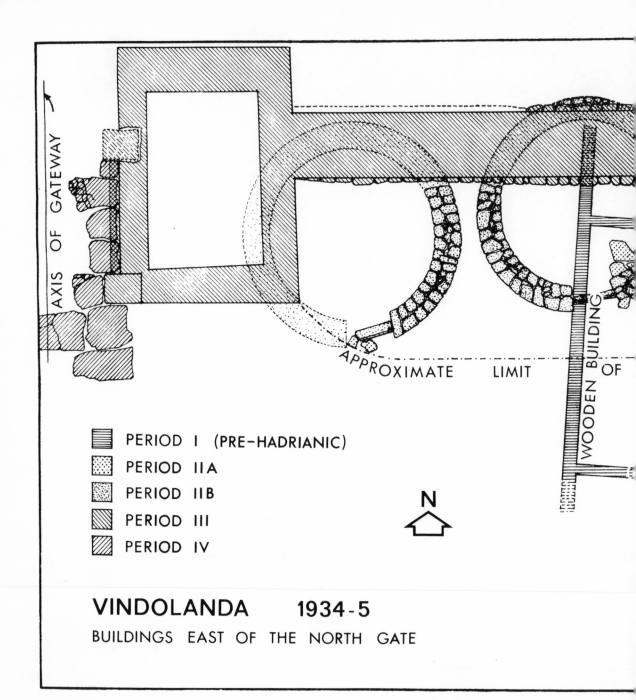

AXIS OF GATEWAY

APPROXIMATE LIMIT

WOODEN BUILDING OF

PERIOD I (PRE-HADRIANIC)
PERIOD IIA
PERIOD IIB
PERIOD III
PERIOD IV

N

VINDOLANDA   1934-5
BUILDINGS EAST OF THE NORTH GATE

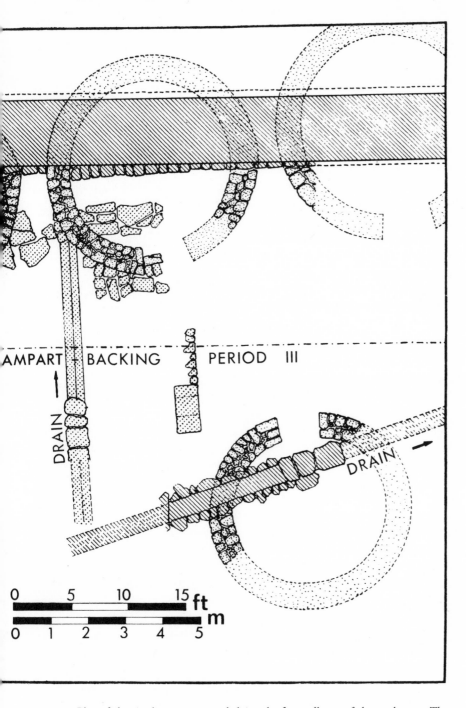

AMPART + BACKING   PERIOD III

DRAIN

DRAIN

0   5   10   15 ft

0   1   2   3   4   5 m

24 *Plan of the circular structures underlying the fort wall east of the north gate. The excavators of the 1930s could ascertain neither the date nor the function of these curious buildings, though their position beneath the stone fort and above pre-Hadrianic wooden structures suggests that they were erected sometime in the mid-second century*

other catapult platforms at all the corners of the fort, but proof must await further research.

The fort gateways

The fort gateways remind us that Vindolanda was not a Hadrianic construction. Reference to the plan shows that only two gates possessed guard-chambers, whilst the east and west gates do not even lie opposite each other. Instead of the elaborate and usually blocked-up twin portals of the Wall forts, a single carriageway alone sufficed here, and the evidence of Anthony Hedley suggests that a flight of stone steps led up to the east gate. The south gate, which I examined and back-filled in 1969,[106] had a distinct step down at the gateway, also debarring wheeled traffic, although in this case, as at the east gate, it is difficult to see where wheeled traffic could have gone to once through the doors.

Recent research in the north-east corner

The only fresh excavation in the stone forts in recent years took place at the north-east corner in 1972. Spells of prolonged bad weather occasionally made it impossible to work in the damp *vicus* field, so I asked the Department of the Environment for permission to examine a stretch of fort wall at the north-east corner, where it might be possible to test the hypothesis that the earlier stone fort extended several feet to the north of the later structure. It was agreed that the surviving masonry would be conserved for display by the Department, should the scale of the discoveries warrant it; otherwise back-filling must take place.

The removal of fallen debris from the fort wall proved to be the answer to the wet-weather problems. The steepness of the slope at this point ensured excellent drainage, and barrowing of spoil was not necessary, since it could be shovelled down the bank. The wall was found to be well hidden in the bank, standing 9 courses high with a further 3–4 feet of core standing above that: sadly, 6 or 7 courses had fallen away since the first investigation by Anthony Hedley in the early nineteenth century. Signs of reconstruction were immediately obvious. The first wall was faced with large, soft sandstone blocks, of similar quality to those in the military bath-houses and early *principia*, but it had been substantially rebuilt more than once. At some stage, a section of the lower masonry had been taken down to ground level in order to insert twin flagged drains through the wall. There was no indication that the earlier wall extended farther north.

Plate 51

With the fort plateau 12 feet above this now weak masonry, and with the drains blocked up, it was essential to take the pressure off the wall and release any water trapped inside. A narrow trench was accordingly inserted on the inner face, and we were rewarded with a fine piece of Roman masonry, 17 courses of stone, 11 feet high, above well-laid flags. Further investigation showed that we had descended into the latrine sewers, for we found the north-east corner of the central platform, similar to that in the fine latrine at Housesteads, 5 feet higher than the sewer bottom. The sewers had become choked with rubbish, mainly bone, but they also contained several examples of Huntcliff ware, the dominant pottery of the post-AD 367 period.

Sadly, the Department of the Environment felt unable to allow us to complete the examination of this latrine, pointing out that their labour force on the Wall, which was to do the conservation, was already fully committed to more essential work, so the open trench had to be back-filled. It was possible, though, to conserve the short stretch of fort wall with the drains, which now serve to remind us how fine these remains would look if only all the walls could be uncovered.

The western ditch

The western ditch of the fort has been sectioned three times during recent excavations, and it is notable for its irregularities. Any deep trenches at Vindolanda present difficulties due to the high water-table, and however efficient a pumping system is employed there is always a film of thick mud at the bottom of a trench. The early sections, dug in 1967 and 1972, showed a ditch which varied between 16 and 20 feet wide, with a steeper slope on the inner face, but with none of the regularity normally so distinctive of Roman ditches. The reasons for this only became apparent in 1973, when it was discovered that both banks had been artificially built up with rubble and clay to cover the posts of the early wooden forts protruding through the sides of the ditch. The most significant information, however, proved to be that this ditch was little more than a drainage channel by the end of the fourth century, having been encroached upon both by the widening of the civilian roadway and by the mass of rubbish thrown into it, especially near the south-west angle of the fort walls. Elsewhere, and especially in the south of England, ditches tend to become wider and deeper in the fourth century, as though to emphasize the uncertainties of the political situation. The absence of such a defence at Vindolanda might suggest a more peaceful way of life, resulting perhaps from the decline in the military importance of the fort. We should not, however, forget the evidence cited in the previous chapter for the increased use of weapons in the fourth-century *vicus*.

The rubbish which choked this ditch included very large quantities of both bone and leather, analysis of which will prove exceptionally valuable

Fig. 25

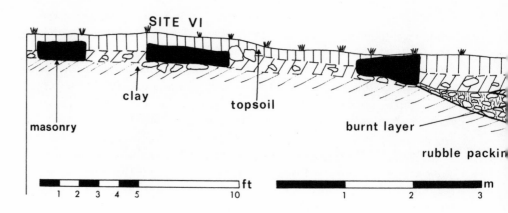

SITE VI

clay

topsoil

masonry

burnt layer

rubble packir

as a comparison with the similar material from the sealed early levels. It is clear, for example, that there was less deer bone here, and the shoes are of a very different style. Other material from the ditch included a stylus tablet with ink writing (although this might have been dislodged during the construction of the ditch from the underlying timber levels), a complete bronze drinking vessel which someone must have dropped accidentally into the foul-smelling water, a shale lathe-end, and a comprehensive assortment of ironmongery. Here, as in the pre-Hadrianic deposits, the wet conditions and the presence of vivianite (ferrous phosphate) seem to have ensured the preservation of much more Roman material than is normal.

Plate X

Future work

There is no doubt that further work inside the stone forts would be immensely rewarding. Substantial remains of the Theodosian occupation may still exist beneath the turf and these could indicate who garrisoned the fort in the late fourth century, whether or not civilians now lived within the fort walls, and how long soldiers actually remained on the site. Below the Theodosian floors the barrack buildings of the Fourth Cohort of Gauls ought to remain in a good state of preservation, undamaged by nineteenth-century exploration. They might give us the information we so badly need about the strength of the regiment in the third century and in the early years of the fourth. The most fascinating period of all, however, is that contemporary with the unusual *principia* with its *adobe* construction: was the fort then also the home of the Fourth Cohort of Gauls, or did it serve some special function? Work on these three levels, inside the $3\frac{1}{2}$ acres of the

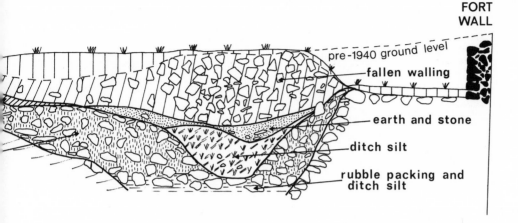

FORT
WALL

pre-1940 ground level

fallen walling

earth and stone

ditch silt

rubble packing and
ditch silt

25 *Section cut in 1973 across the fort ditch immediately to the north of the causeway by the west gate (see site plan, fig. 4). Wet weather and the high water-table combined to prevent the completion of the work, and it is likely that pre-Hadrianic remains survive here in as good condition as they do farther south*

stone fort, could keep a full-time excavation team usefully employed for twenty years, and their task would still not be done. For below the three stone periods lie at least four more periods of occupation, well sealed and probably as well preserved as the early remains we shall now turn to.

IV Terracotta head, perhaps a portrait of a deity, found in the ditch off the south-western corner of the stone fort. The traces of black paint on the face hint at a North African origin, possibly during the reign of the first African emperor, Severus (AD 193–211).

V Bronze coins found in the latrine sewer of the military bath-house.

VI Miscellaneous jewellery and toilet items from the civilian settlements: bronze cockerel (cf. plate 18), jet betrothal medallion (cf. plates 46, 47), beads, bangle, pins, rings, bone and copper-alloy hairpins, tweezers and stone palette.

VII Bronze belt attachments with enamelled inlays from the civilian settlements.

VIII Rings and gemstones found in the recent excavations at Vindolanda. Note in particular the Medusa head ring in the middle of the back row (cf. plate 19) and the red jasper intaglios in the foreground (cf. plates 34–41).

IX The headquarters building (*principia*) of the stone fort, looking east towards Barcombe Hill, from whose summit the Romans quarried much of the stone for their forts. In the foreground stands the commanding officer's rostrum (*tribunal*), and behind it, various administrative rooms.

X A bronze drinking vessel found at the bottom of the ditch off the south-western corner of the late stone fort.

XI Excavations in progress in 1973 at the level of the period III pre-Hadrianic fort, beneath the later stone civilian structures of sites II and III (cf. *fig. 28*). Note the well-preserved wattle fencing in the centre of the picture.

XII Two bronze trumpet brooches from the pre-Hadrianic deposits.

IV

V

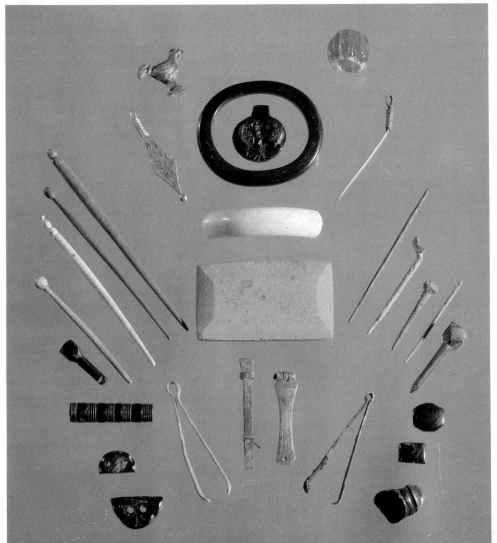

VI

VII

VIII

IX

X

XI

XII

VI The pre-Hadrianic forts

Discovery and excavation

When Eric Birley undertook excavation at Vindolanda in 1930, one of his objectives was to locate evidence for occupation of the site before the construction of Hadrian's Wall, in part to determine whether the fort had been founded as early as Agricola's governorship, and in part to see whether information from the earliest levels could help date the initial Roman withdrawal from Scotland. He duly located ditches and a rampart of an early fort in the north-western part of the site later occupied by the civilian settlement, and discovered more evidence for timber buildings of the same period below the north rampart of the stone forts.[107] The small scale of his work (which was largely concerned with the later history of the site) gave neither a firm date for this early occupation nor an indication of the size of the fort, although Trajanic material was definitely present. Similar early deposits were sampled in 1967 and 1968,[108] with little conclusive result, and the decision of 1970 to concentrate upon the *vicus* ruled out any immediate attempt to investigate the early remains.

Fig. 26

The subsequent discovery of the extraordinary remains of the pre-Hadrianic forts was purely fortuitous. The excavations of 1971 and 1972 in the heart of the *vicus* had interrupted both the natural drainage and several farmers' pipe-drains, and during heavy rain great pools of water built up in the exposed buildings fronting the west wall of the stone fort. It seemed sensible to lay a new 6-inch pipe, if possible, to clear this water down the south slope and into the Doe Sike, but it was essential to avoid disturbance to Roman structures. Accordingly, in the difficult southern stretch of the pipeline, I selected a curving course running between two civilian buildings which I had excavated in February 1959, in the part of the field which was not even scheduled as an ancient monument.[109] Towards the end of August 1972 half-a-dozen volunteers joined me in this mundane task, driving a 3-foot-wide trench down through the iron slag which lay outside the small foundry (site II). Below the slag there was a hard brown clay, which in 1959 we had taken to be the natural subsoil, and the lie of the land demanded that the pipe be laid at least 3 feet below the top of this material. The slag was as hard as concrete, some 14 inches thick, and it was a relief to strike the less durable clay beneath. Everything proceeded according to plan, until the clay disappeared after a little less than 3 feet and a mass of black, organic material, similar to pond growth, was encountered. The trench immediately filled with water, and morale amongst the ditch-diggers began to fall. The introduction of a pump improved matters, and the drainage trench began to progress downwards. It must be appreciated that we were digging a part of the site which had already been excavated, and which lay well outside the known position of the early forts, on the very fringes of the later civilian settlement. Moreover, to the best of our knowledge, we were digging down through glacial clay. With only 6 inches more depth to dig out, one of the volunteers suddenly produced a gleaming piece of South Gaulish Samian ware from the black filth at his feet – and the course of the excavations was altered in dramatic fashion.

The thick layer of clay, tightly packed and exceptionally clean, was not natural subsoil, for it concealed a thick deposit of occupation material of undoubted pre-Hadrianic date. In the narrow drainage trench it was impossible to bottom the deposit, and the season was drawing to a close. But the early South Gaulish Samian was followed by numerous other pieces of pottery, leather, fragments of wood, and three pieces of Roman textile in magnificent condition, so it was essential that we should return to this area in 1973 to determine the nature of the deposit.

The early spring of 1973 was both warm and dry, and it was possible for the permanent staff to resume outdoor work early in March. The drainage trench was re-opened and enlarged, since it was important to discover whether the finds of 1972 had come from a pit or ditch, and whether there was any trace of structures. Within a fortnight, a 10-foot square had been opened up, building posts discovered *in situ*, and the deposit bottomed at a depth of 13 feet from the surface. In that time, the first writing tablets were found (see chapter VIII), and the special measures necessary to deal with the extraordinary deposit had been worked out.

Two particular physical problems had to be overcome. Working to depths of 13 feet required special equipment – timber shoring, safety helmets, ladders, pumps and so on – and it involved the lifting and removal of countless buckets of sifted earth and debris. But the major problem was that of water. The natural water-table appeared to lie at a mere 3 feet 9 inches (the reason for this was only discovered later, see below), and once that depth was reached, water seeped in through the sides of the trench and bubbled up through the floor. The working area quickly became a quagmire, every feature and find assuming the same muddy colour. It was essential to dig a sump, 2–3 feet deeper than the desired working floor and about 2 feet square, from which a suction pump could remove the water every few minutes. Overnight, in dry weather, the trench normally accumulated about 3 feet of water, which might take an hour to pump out

Figs. 39, 40

Plate XI

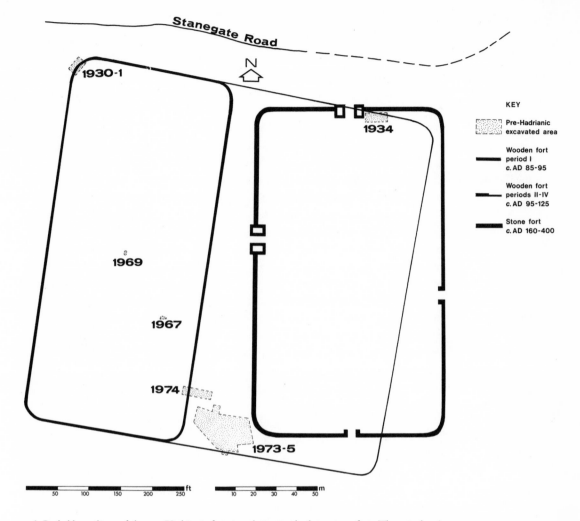

N

1930-1

1934

1969

1967

1974

1973-5

KEY

Pre-Hadrianic
excavated area

Wooden fort
period I
c. AD 85-95

Wooden fort
periods II-IV
c. AD 95-125

Stone fort
c. AD 160-400

ft
50   100   150   200   250

m
10   20   30   40   50

26 *Probable outlines of the pre-Hadrianic forts in relation to the later stone fort. The actual pre-Hadrianic areas excavated are shown stippled, together with dates of excavation. For the 1934 area, see fig. 24; for the 1973–5 area, see figs. 28, 29 and 30; for the 1974 area, see figs. 27 and 32–5*

before work could begin. In wet weather, when the trench became the natural drainage point for the surrounding land, it might take the whole morning to clear the water. Whatever problems there might be in such an excavation, the efficient dispersal of water was the crucial factor, and the mechanical pump became our most valued piece of equipment.

Once the writing tablets had been discovered, trowelling of the floors had to be abandoned, since with a trowel it was virtually impossible to find the tablets without damaging them. Instead we cut the flooring into cubes, approximately 8 inches by 8 inches and 6 inches deep, and then passed these up to the surface where they were peeled apart by hand. Later

Figs. 33–35

refinements improved this system, so that by mid-1974 we had adopted the procedure of laying out a 12-inch grid over the horizontal floor levels, numbering each sod and recording its contents individually for plotting on the site plan. In this way, it was possible to see how much rubbish had accumulated over the years on a Roman floor.

Another technique we had to develop was that of excavating trenches which narrowed very slightly as they were dug deeper. We discovered that the exposed organic matter – up to 8 feet deep in places – retained its range of distinctive colours (predominantly green, yellow and shades of brown) for as little as ten minutes in hot weather, and thereafter reverted to a matt black. In other words, if a trench was excavated to a depth of 13 feet in a matter of three or four weeks, the sides would reveal nothing of the stratigraphy when it was time to draw the section. It would be necessary to remove another 6 inches or so of the side walls to recover the colours and produce a meaningful drawing, but this might cause trench collapse if initially the sides had been made straight. We therefore adopted the procedure of cutting trenches with inward-sloping walls, making them vertical only when section drawing became essential.

Plates 60–82

It took some time to create the form of organization described above, and we had to learn by experience. The first task was to seek help on a large scale. The conservation of the writing tablets, the thousands of leather items, the wooden objects and the textiles was more than any single conservation officer could cope with, and at that time (1973) even the North of England Museum Service was without conservation facilities. Through the good offices of Mr Richard Wright and Dr A. E. A. Werner, the tablets were accepted by the British Museum Research Laboratory, while Professor Barri Jones undertook to conserve the leather and wood in Manchester. Without the aid of these scholars, the situation would have been critical. Now that the Trust has its own museum, the finds can be treated on the site, using the techniques developed so successfully in London and Manchester.

The cost of all this work was necessarily large, and it was soon evident that all the 1973 funds would be exhausted by one small excavation in the early deposits. At this stage the *Observer* newspaper came to our aid, providing sufficient money for a further six weeks' work. The ensuing newspaper articles did much to boost the number of visitors to Vindolanda, further helping the funds, and they served to put us in touch with many more environmental specialists anxious to see the remarkable deposits.

TRENCH A4.75 SECTION a/b

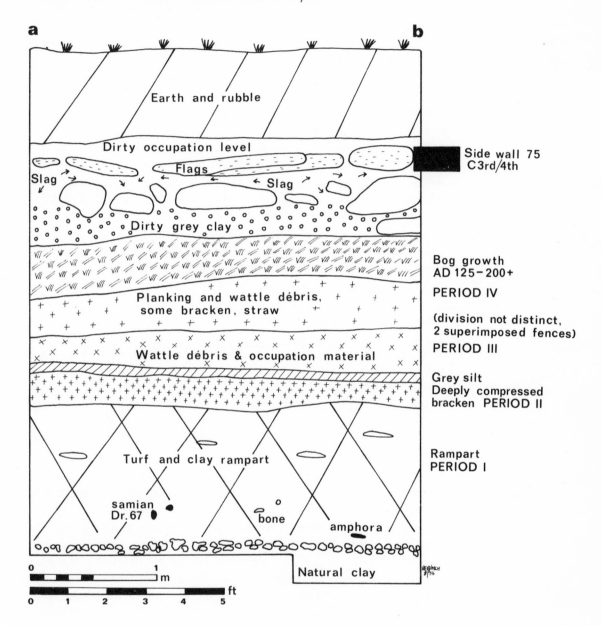

27 Section a/b across the eastern end of trench A4.75, excavated in 1974, showing the relationship of the pre-Hadrianic military deposits (periods I–IV) to the civilian occupational levels of the third and fourth centuries

The pre-Hadrianic deposits

Fig. 27

The section drawing for the 1974 trench (A4. 75) shows the relationship of the early deposits to the later civilian buildings. The great depth of the early material is not encountered everywhere on the site, and may be explained here as the result of the gradual levelling of a natural depression, with, as a consequence, less disturbance than normal of earlier structures when rebuilding took place. The uppermost timber structure (period IV) had been demolished by the Romans in about AD 125 and left to rot in a quickly forming swamp, so that a 12-inch deposit of bog growth had developed by the time the civilian builders came to seal it with clay. Beneath sites II and

Fig. 29

III only isolated stumps remained of period IV buildings, for here this level was encountered by later Roman ditch-diggers and ruthlessly destroyed. (Water still flowed along this ditch in modern times, hence our erroneous assumption in 1959 that we had reached the natural water-table).

Fig. 28

The block plan of the 1973–5 excavations indicates the comparatively small scale of the work carried out in relation to the area of the site, and the restrictions imposed by the foundations of later stone structures. In 1973 a 20-yard length of flagged roadway was removed together with two walls of site III, but the stones were planned and numbered before the demolition and can be replaced once the in-fill has settled. The elucidation of the history of the site during the timber periods was exceptionally complicated, but by the end of the 1975 season most of the uncertainties had been removed.

The first phase, period I, was represented by the turf rampart and ditch of a fort which had later been levelled; none of its buildings were examined. The construction of a new and larger fort was indicated by the substantial remains of a *fabrica* or workshop, which was subsequently reconstructed on the same site: these periods we know as IIa and IIb. There followed a major change, with the comprehensive demolition of all structures and the levelling of the site, before a new wooden building, of a different type and plan, was constructed and soon after substantially rebuilt, giving us periods IIIa and IIIb. Finally, these remains were also levelled and another timber structure (period IV), was laid out; little of the building, however, survived the work of the industrious ditch-diggers.

Although it is doubtful whether we will ever be able to date these periods with absolute precision, or discover the reasons for the many changes, the outside limits for building activity and abandonment are secure. In theory, period I might just pre-date the arrival of Agricola in the north (*c.* AD 78–9), but this is most unlikely, and a date in the early 80s seems fairly certain. Periods IIa and IIb, on the evidence of coins (Domitian and Trajan) and the dated writing tablet (*c.* AD 103, see chapter VIII), lie within

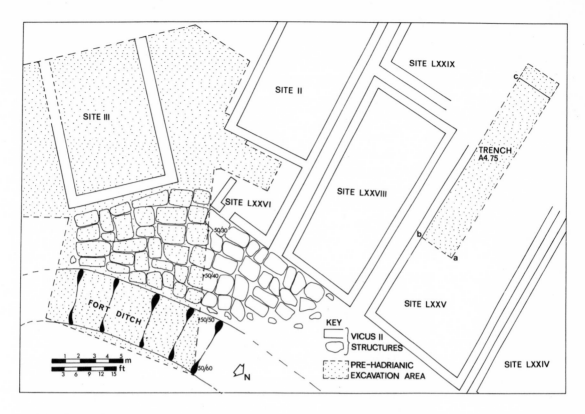

28 Plan showing the pre-Hadrianic excavation areas of 1973–5 in relation to the later structures of the civilian settlement. For section 50/30–50/77 and its associated plan, see figs. 29 and 30 respectively; for plans, section a/b and section b/c of trench A4.75, see figs. 33–5, 27 and 32 respectively

the years AD 95–105, and the remaining periods must fall between AD 105 and 125 (period III probably 105–20, period IV 120–5), by which time the garrison ought to have been ready to move into its new Wall fort at Housesteads. A fragmentary address on one of the writing tablets implies that Vindolanda's garrison from AD 95 was the First Cohort of Tungrians, who are known to have been at Housesteads in the third and fourth centuries. There was no trace in any period of destruction, either by accidental fire or enemy action, and other reasons must be found for the alterations that were carried out. The difference in size between the periods I and II forts (*c.* 3½ and 8 acres respectively) suggests a change in the composition of the garrison, perhaps with a regiment 500 strong being replaced by another 1,000 strong, or an infantry regiment giving way to cavalry. Reconstruction at regular intervals was inevitable when the chief building material was timber, and since the birchwood used at Vindolanda was left unseasoned its life may have been little more than five years. The despatch of a detachment for duties elsewhere or the temporary

Fig. 26

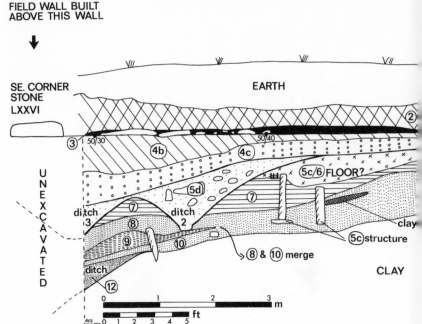

SECTION SA 50/30 – 50/77

29 The complicated 1975 section for the 'fabrica trench' (fig. 30), showing the position of the three later ditches of the stone forts which removed much of the periods III and IV pre-Hadrianic structures and created a suspended water-table

assimilation of men from another regiment would also have required immediate changes in the layout of a fort. The late first century and the early years of the second century were notorious for the frequency of new regimental postings, which may account for the alterations that took place at Vindolanda between periods II and III *c.* AD 105. The period IV structure appears to have been the work of some more humble unit, drafted into the area for menial duties during the construction of the Wall.

Periods IIa, IIIa and IIIb were sufficiently well preserved to give us useful information regarding Roman timber construction. The below-floor foundation timbers were discovered *in situ*, since demolition had involved merely the axing down of uprights to floor level. Thus stumps of major uprights remained morticed into their beam slots and wattling still wove in and out of the intervening minor timbers. The period I rampart, standing to a height of 4 feet when excavated despite levelling, showed also how the Roman builders gave added support to a turf structure. A full section through the south rampart demonstrated, too late for our use on the replica construction (see chapter IX), that the Romans were aware of the problems

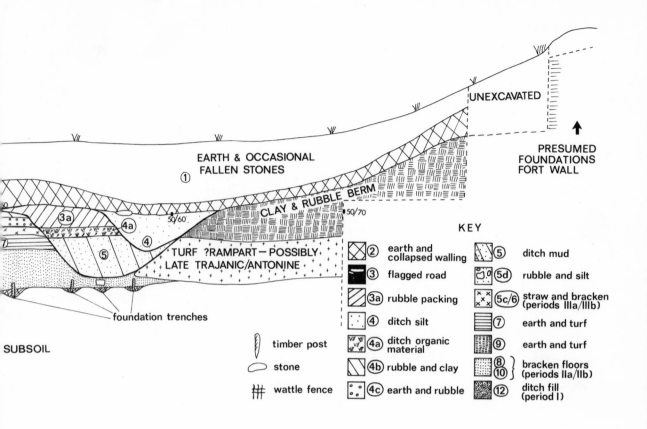

EARTH & OCCASIONAL FALLEN STONES ①

PRESUMED FOUNDATIONS FORT WALL

UNEXCAVATED

CLAY & RUBBLE BERM

TURF ?RAMPART — POSSIBLY LATE TRAJANIC/ANTONINE

foundation trenches

SUBSOIL

KEY

⊠②	earth and collapsed walling
■③	flagged road
▨③a	rubble packing
④	ditch silt
④a	ditch organic material
④b	rubble and clay
④c	earth and rubble
⑤	ditch mud
⑤d	rubble and silt
5c/6	straw and bracken (periods IIIa/IIIb)
⑦	earth and turf
⑨	earth and turf
⑧⑩	bracken floors (periods IIa/IIb)
⑫	ditch fill (period I)

timber post

stone

wattle fence

of such defences. The lack of moisture and therefore grass growth on the southern side was compensated for by additional features: horizontal layers of timber laid north-south helped to bind the structure together, and, whilst the main body of the rampart was turf, the southern face was reinforced with clay and a stone base.

The period IIa building was almost certainly part of a *fabrica* or workshop to judge by its contents (see next chapter), although its general position within the ramparts does not make it clear whether this was the regimental workshop or a smaller affair attached to another building, such as the commanding officer's residence. The IIa structure was surrounded by an unusual wattle drain, which at first was mistaken for an earlier structural period until an intact section was discovered in 1975, confirming that the twin wattle fences, 12 inches apart, had once been roofed with wattle as well. Such wattle-work was also used for the side walls of buildings, where the interior faces would be plastered with a clay-and-straw daub and perhaps painted. The use of the same material for drains implies the expenditure of a major proportion of time and energy upon the collection

Fig. 30

Plates 52, 53

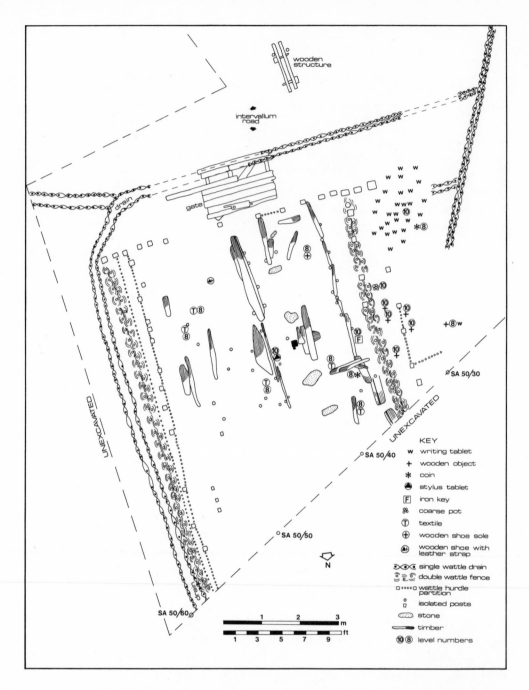

KEY

w	writing tablet
+	wooden object
*	coin
◓	stylus tablet
F	iron key
⚭	coarse pot
T	textile
⊕	wooden shoe sole
◒	wooden shoe with leather strap
⟨⟩⟨⟩	single wattle drain
⟨⟩⟨⟩	double wattle fence
⊡••••	wattle hurdle partition
° □	isolated posts
⟨⟩	stone
⟨—⟩	timber
⑩⑧	level numbers

30 Plan of the pre-Hadrianic area beneath the flagged road and part of site III, showing periods IIa and IIb (levels 8 and 10). The structures visible have been interpreted as the remains of a workshop (fabrica) connected with leather tanning, judging by the debris on the floors (see chapter VII). The majority of the writing tablets came from these deposits, and in this context must represent rubbish thrown out from another room. Cf. plates 52–3, 55–7. For section SA50/30–50/77 see fig. 29

31 A horizontal beam slot for the uprights of a period IIIa building

of birch branches and their weaving into suitable pre-fabricated sections, similar to those in use today in some parts of the country as sheep-pens. It is surprising that a fort near the later site of Hadrian's Wall made no use whatever of dressed stone, even in its drains, and it suggests that the construction of the Wall revolutionized the army's building methods and necessitated much retraining of specialists.

The building techniques of the successive structures varied considerably. The period IIa structure had been laid out with a 2-foot-wide construction trench, 16 inches deep, and wattle side walls had been set against each trench edge, while the interior, at ground level, was filled with puddled clay. The inner wall appeared to be stronger than the outer, with squared 4-inch-by-4-inch posts every 5 feet or so, smaller circular posts every foot and wattle-work woven between all of them. The outer wall possessed no squared timbers; instead circular posts at 2-foot intervals carried the weight of the wattle-work. Period IIb saw no change in building techniques, but both periods IIIa and IIIb were quite different. In IIIa, the builders constructed the main frame of their structure with squared uprights, 6 inches by 6 inches, morticed into short, pre-fabricated lengths of horizontal sleeper beams, and with substantial circular posts between the main timbers at intervals of 1 foot; birch branches were then woven round all the timbers. The IIIb building which soon succeeded this structure reverted to the foundation-trench method, but instead of a clay filling between wattle

Plate 52; *fig. 30*

Plate 54

113

TRENCH A4.75 SECTION b/c

32 Section b/c along the southern edge of trench A4.75, revealing the major north-south rampart of period I (cf. Figs. 26-7). The second-century bog growth was particularly marked in this area, the wettest part of the site

fences huge uprights had been driven into the ground at 15-foot intervals, with smaller squared uprights (5 inches by 4 inches) set on thin stone base-plates at intervals of slightly more than 2 feet. The foundation trench was then packed solid with rough, undressed sandstone, and a very distinctive, thin wattle fence, with narrow uprights every $1\frac{1}{2}$ inches, ran along the inner face of the main timbers. In each case, great efforts had been made to salvage the main uprights on the demolition of the buildings. Many had been axed down at floor level, but some had been withdrawn entirely, and the wattle fencing had been removed, probably for burning off the site.

The differing construction techniques may reflect the functions of the buildings. IIa and IIb, as workshops, were utilitarian: IIIa and IIIb, serving some different purpose as yet undiscovered, were more pretentious and imposing. On the other hand, the changes may reflect the varied customs of different regiments, and we must look closely at the writing tablets, with their scrawled addresses on the outsides, to see whether they hint at troop movements.

The condition of the flooring inside the buildings varied almost as much as did the construction technique. IIa and IIb possessed bracken and straw floors, reinforced by domestic and industrial refuse, lying upon a spread of clay, although IIa also included a series of unshaped boulders, set more or less in a line, down the middle of the principal room. IIIa's floor had been severely damaged during the later insertion of the IIIb structure, but where

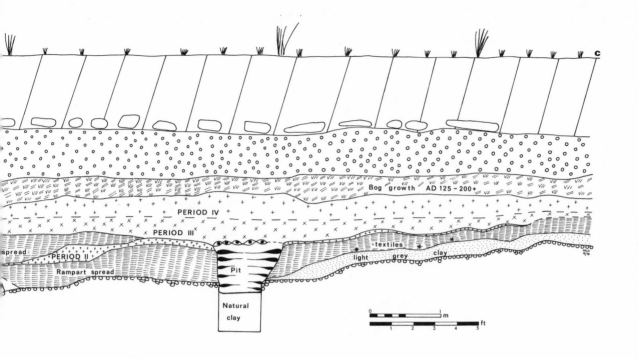

PERIOD IV

PERIOD III

PERIOD II

Bog growth AD 125 - 200+

textiles

light grey clay

spread

Rampart spread

Pit

Natural clay

0   1 m

1   2   3   4   5 ft

it survived it consisted of a clay base and a scatter of straw, with two patches of wooden planking, laid directly on to the clay. Only IIIb contained a stone floor, consisting of boulders and unshaped freestone packed together in clay to form an exceptionally solid if uneven surface, upon which bracken and straw had then been laid. Experience of later Roman construction on the site, when the use of heavy and regular flagstones was almost universal, leaves one astonished that the otherwise highly efficient early military garrison did not quarry proper stones from the many suitable outcrops nearby, but resorted instead to collecting unpromising material from stream-beds. It is further confirmation that the trade of the mason was still in its infancy amongst the auxiliary troops on the frontier.

A surprising discovery was a large timber gate lying outside the *fabrica*, on a slightly raised stone platform at the edge of the intervallum road. The gate was already old and much patched when it was set down in position, and may have served as the base for a water tank or immersion container connected with leather tanning. Its frame below the face timbers was well preserved, but the planking had been shattered by the weight pressing down on to the uneven supports.

Plates 56, 57

Trench A4.75

In 1974 a small section was dug some 80 feet to the north-west of the buildings described above, to determine whether the unusual conditions of

Figs. 27, 32–35

KEY

O	coarse pottery fragment
●	samian fragment
■	bone
□	tooth
▲	leather object
△	leather fragment
I	hazel nut
ⓦ	walnut
⋈	oyster shell
Ⓢ	stable fly pupae
c	charcoal
Ⓒ	coal
G	glass
T	tile
w	ink writing tablet
+	wooden object
r	string
R	rope
L	lead
N	iron nail
⊕	stylus tablet
⊙	stylus tablet wood
B	bronze instrument
⊛	silver ring with intaglio
⊕	wooden comb
—	mortarium
⊞	bronze stud
⊿	bronze fragment
✳	melon bead
⊙	iron peg
⊘	iron stud
⊡	bronze object
▷	bone dice
⊚	bone gaming counter
⊛	crucible fragment

preservation found in 1973 extended much farther. It produced important information for the later timber periods, for it was beyond the range of the stone fort's ditch-diggers, and the final period was undamaged. There was clear evidence that a structure abandoned in period IV had become immersed in a swamp before civilian building commenced on the site much later, and brushwood, predominantly birch and hawthorn, had achieved a substantial hold. This scrub had been axed flat by the civilian builders and sealed below a thick spread of clay. The position of the 1974 trench was such that any structures found could not belong to the complex farther

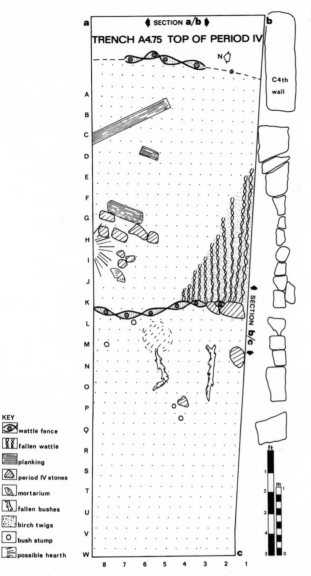

KEY
- 🌀 wattle fence
- 🗙🗙 fallen wattle
- ▤ planking
- ◈ period IV stones
- ◈ mortarium
- ◭ fallen bushes
- ⬚ birch twigs
- ○ bush stump
- ▥ possible hearth

33–35 Plans of three different levels in the 1974 pre-Hadrianic excavation area, on the site of a probable barrack building. The extraordinary quantity and variety of rubbish deposited on the floors can be seen by reference to the key. For sections a/b and b/c, see figs. 27 and 32 respectively

south (the *fabrica* trench), and it was apparent that the nature of the flooring was also different. Although both the periods III and IV floors contained some bracken, the principal ingredient was straw, and the period II floors, almost exclusively of bracken, were much thinner than those elsewhere, as though the room had been cleaned out at regular intervals. But this area also contained writing tablets, although fewer in number than in the *fabrica* trench, and one example (no. 129: see chapter VIII) from the period IV floor seemed to be a letter addressed to a private soldier. The period IV building may well have been a barrack.

XIII Two fragmentary leaves of a writing tablet (no. 29), part of a letter of recommendation addressed to a man named Cerialis, probably the commanding officer of Vindolanda at the time (before c. AD 105). The faces of the leaves with writing were found stuck together. For a translation of the text, see chapter VIII.

XIV A fragment of woollen textile from the pre-Hadrianic deposits.

XV The replicas of Hadrian's Wall, including the stone turret, completed in 1974.

XIII
XIV

XV

Conclusion

It must be stressed that the scope of the work carried out on the early levels was very small. The abundance of the finds tends to conceal the limitations of the plans obtained from the excavations. We are little wiser, for instance, about the layout of these forts, and we cannot even be certain which way they faced. Nevertheless the main purpose of the research was to establish a reliable chronology for the pre-Hadrianic occupation, and in this we were largely successful. In particular, the existence of four major timber periods was established, spanning the years pre-AD 90–125, which suggests that the early history of the fort was remarkably similar to that of the military complex at Corbridge, half a day's march to the east. (Corbridge apparently had at least four successive timber forts confined to the period AD 90–125 and underlying second-to-fourth-century stone structures. Some believe that an earlier, Agricolan fort had once existed to the west, at the Red Burn site).

It will be many years before a meaningful plan of the early forts can be produced, and it is arguable that it may be unwise to attempt such a task, since it must inevitably involve severe damage to the substantial later stone structures. But perhaps the most severe drawback to further work is the huge volume of material that will be found in any such excavation, as the following chapters will demonstrate.

VII The finds from the pre-Hadrianic forts

The occupation floors of the early military buildings and the ditch fill of the first fort yielded an astonishing collection of Roman artifacts and environmental produce, preserved in a magnificent state. The flooring of the period II *fabrica* or workshop contained the most unusual material. The flooring consisted of bracken and patches of straw and moss, spread evenly over a clay floor. Additional covering had at times been laid down on top of the old mat, producing ultimately a compacted organic carpet up to 14 inches thick. The high water-table and the low-lying ground ensured that the floor remained damp (although not water-logged) even in the Roman period. Dr Mark Seaward, who is analysing the environmental evidence at the site, has concluded that the heavy concentration of damp bracken sealed by clay, together with iron phosphate (vivianite) derived from the bones, generated a chemical reaction which preserved the contents, however perishable, in almost perfect condition. When a cut was made into this material, breaking the seal and allowing oxygen to reach the vegetable matter, the process of decay was rapid, and the sickly smell at the bottom of a poorly ventilated trench was enough to induce sickness in the most hardened excavator.

Food remains

The period II deposit contained a variety of material which is difficult to associate together, and must represent accumulated rubbish from other rooms, tipped on to this floor to dry damp patches or make it firmer. There was a variety of food litter: the broken-up bones of cattle and sheep, pigs, horses, deer, dogs, hare and fowl, together with numerous oysters and mussel shells and some bones of a cat and of a bird larger than museum specimens of goose or swan. There were also thousands of hazel-nut shells and a few imported walnut shells. Clearly somewhere nearby good food had been consumed, but there was little pottery in this deposit, and the few examples of mixing bowls (*mortaria*) and cooking pots, with one exception, had obviously been broken elsewhere.

Plates 58, 59

Mr George Hodgson, who has studied the animal bones, deduces from the kill-patterns that all the principal food-bearing animals – mainly cattle,

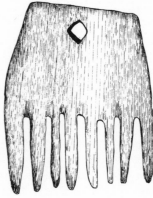

36 Two wooden objects from the fabrica or workshop that were almost certainly used in the leather-tanning process. (Left) One of numerous half-moon-shaped objects for scraping fat off skins, about 6 inches wide. (Right) A box-wood carding comb, 4¾ inches long

but also sheep, goats, pigs, horses and deer – were reared primarily for meat, although cattle, sheep and goats would in addition have provided milk and cheese, as well as other secondary products such as leather, wool or hair.[110] As might have been expected, the animals were much smaller than their modern counterparts, with the exception of the deer; sheep in particular would have produced only an insignificant quantity of meat. A comparison of the bones from this early deposit with those found in the fourth-century fort's ditch suggests that the Romans successfully improved the size of their cattle by selective breeding in the course of the occupation.

Tanning and leatherwork

A second category of bone had nothing to do with domestic cooking. The complete skulls of oxen, sheep, goats, horses and dogs were found together with an exceptionally large number of foot and hoof bones, which included those of numerous deer. This was the kind of refuse one might associate with a tannery: the main carcass would have left the slaughterhouse for the regimental stores, and the hide, with head and legs attached, would have been sent to the tannery. A number of wooden items could also have belonged to leatherworkers. There were fourteen half-moon-shaped pieces of wood, similar to the instruments used in more modern times to scrape the fat off skins, together with over twenty fine box-wood combs, of the sort one would associate with fashionable women's hair. One example which still contained hair was sent to the

Fig. 36

Plate 60

North-western Forensic Laboratory,[111] where examination showed it to be coarse, textured animal hair of a dark brown-black colour, probably from a cow, and we must conclude that the combs were also used at some stage in the tanning process. Other indicators of tanning or leatherworking were the large wooden vat-stirrer, an iron punch, several knives and a voluminous collection of leather offcuts. The most compelling evidence, however, was revealed by Dr Seaward's analysis of the organic material in the floors: he discovered, much to his surprise (at this stage, in 1973, leatherworking had not been considered), evidence for heavy urination and patches of excreta.[112] Taken out of context, in the middle of an excavation season, Dr Seaward's evidence caused a ripple of shock in Romano-British archaeological circles, for it was thought that the building was part of the commanding officer's residence, and the presence of urine and excreta in the filthy floors of a Roman military building was utterly at variance with the traditional picture of cleanliness and good order. But Dr Seaward was not mistaken. Tens of thousands of the pupae of stable flies had been laid amongst this rubbish by discerning insects who knew what they were looking for. Many of these pupae had never hatched, although the young flies were perfectly formed inside, and this raised the question of whether the Romans had developed some method of fumigating the room. It may be, however, that the natural chemicals in the bracken, which can cause cancer in cattle,[113] account for the premature deaths. Whatever the reason, the presence of unborn Roman stable flies is the best possible testimony to the remarkable preservative conditions existing at Vindolanda for this early period. The excreta are difficult to identify with precision, but they were certainly deposited by meat-eaters, probably by dogs or humans.

The presence of urine and excreta in this floor makes the identification of the building as a *fabrica* almost certain. Consultations with leatherworkers revealed that the custom of soaking fresh hides in a festering infusion of urine and excreta, to loosen the hairs and make the hides flexible, was an old-established method which was still practised at the beginning of the twentieth century. Many believe that modern chemicals have yet to achieve as good results, and bemoan the ending of the shipments of dog dung from Turkey. We must therefore assume that the Vindolanda material had spilled out of wooden vats which once stood on the floor of the building or on the gate-platform just outside.

A host of other material had also been deposited on the floors. Besides the off-cuts, there was a wide range of leather goods, including shoes, garments, belts, thongs and a purse, some of which were obviously cast-offs. The footwear was particularly interesting. Of over 200 items found in the pre-Hadrianic levels, 70 per cent were so small that they must have been

Plates 61, 62

Plate 63
Plates 64–66

worn by women and children. This is not the first occasion when excavation within a fort has revealed non-military leatherwork (see especially the finds from Bar Hill on the Antonine Wall in Scotland[114]). Yet there must be a limit to the volume of civilian evidence which we can attribute to the commanding officer's household alone. Eric Birley has argued that centurions may also have been allowed to have their families within the fort walls, and that the flats for centurions attached to the barrack buildings provided ample space for a small household.[115] Even if this theory is correct, however, the volume of female and children's possessions found within forts suggests that the Roman army regulations may never have been strictly applied on some frontiers. Other civilian finds in this context were a bronze pendant ear-ring, four hair-pins and a variety of beads.

The variety of shoe-types was considerable. The most common group was the *calceus*, a boot or shoe with a sole of several thicknesses and with laces which tied at the ankle. Several variants of this type were found, and all were studded with small, flat and round nails, sometimes arranged in a pattern and sometimes hammered in randomly. The *carbatina*, or indoor shoe cut from a single piece of leather, was also popular, and this group contained many items which appear to have been home-made. But there were also three examples of the rare *caliga*-type sandal, a fancy open lattice-work shoe which was principally worn in Italy itself, where the climate suited it better. Of several notable items, the finest was the lady's 'Persian' slipper, recording the name of the manufacturer (Lucius Aebutius Thales, son of Titus), together with stamps of a vine-leaf and *cornucopiae*, which latter are repeated on the inner leaves of the sole. Two more shoes, both too small for adults to wear, bear makers' stamps. The greatest surprise was the collection of four complete or fragmentary wooden slippers, almost identical to those sold under a famous brand-name today. It seems likely

Plate 66
Fig. 37

Fig. 38

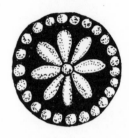

37 A leaf and a rosette stamp from pre-Hadrianic leather shoes, about ⅓ inch across

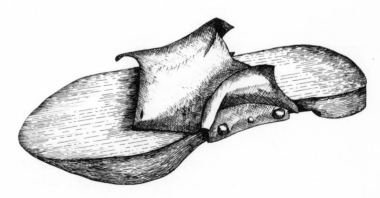

38 One of four wooden bath-house slippers from the period II pre-Hadrianic floor, about 8¼ inches long

that these were bath-house slippers worn by bathers to protect their feet from the hot concrete floors.[116] Similar footwear is still issued to bathers in Turkey today.[117]

Preliminary analysis of the leatherwork, with the invaluable help of Mr J. W. Jackman of Booth International Leather Tanners Ltd, has shown that the footwear was predominantly made from cattle-hides, although the 'Persian' slipper employed goatskin for its uppers and the garments included cattle-hide, goatskin and deerskin. In general, the hides had been tanned to a moderate standard only, and close scrutiny of the finished products revealed some with inefficient de-hairing and more with over-hasty skinning – often the hide had been pierced by the flesher's knife. Despite these imperfections, however, the leather had still been used for garments, with patches sewn over the blemishes. Other hides revealed areas of diseased skin, which were also patched. Only rarely did the thread survive in stitched garments and shoes, but the stitching holes were sometimes so uniform and fine as to suggest that they had been punched out by a machine. In other cases, the garment-maker had been both unskilled and careless, failing to stitch some seams properly and using increasingly large spaces between the stitches. The collection as a whole suggested that there had been two distinct types of product: some 70 per cent of the shoes and garments were clearly the work of craftsmen, and had been well made from good leather; the remaining 30 per cent were extraordinarily amateur, and we must suppose that some people did their own leatherwork.

The writing tablets

Plates 75–82

The floor of the period II building also produced the bulk of the writing tablets, whose significance is discussed in the next chapter. In this context they represent rubbish thrown out of another room: scattered across the floor, and with some bearing traces of burning, they appear to have been dead files destroyed in periodic clean-outs. The tablets themselves were in part the property of the fort's commanding officer, and ought to have reached this room from either his residence or the headquarters building.

Textiles

The special chemical conditions in the period II floor had contributed to the survival of numerous scraps of textile, although those lying near the bottom of the floor were usually heavily rotted. In the three seasons over 100 examples were found, providing a corpus of information almost as unexpected as that of the writing tablets. Ancient textile fabrics and the methods used to produce them are poorly documented, yet the mere fact that the inhabitants of the Roman empire wore clothes ensured that the textile industry played an important role in the Roman economic system. The accidents of survival have usually dealt harshly with textiles, and the archaeologist in Western Europe only rarely comes across the remains of what must have been an industry of greater importance than, say, pottery, whose survivals dominate most archaeological sites. Bog conditions, especially in Scandinavia, and very dry climates, such as in the Middle East, are normally the only environments in which textile remains have been found, although petrified fragments have occasionally turned up on British sites. The great majority of finds from Western Europe have come from the wet rubbish heaps of Mainz, in Germany.[118] The Vindolanda examples, which have doubled our collection of Roman textiles, are therefore of special importance.

All the Vindolanda textiles were found either in the floor of the period II *fabrica* or in the fill of the period I ditch. Where they lay amongst the compressed bracken, they were still strong enough to handle, and required only gentle washing and pressing. Preliminary research on the first group found in 1973 enabled Dr Martin Ryder, who has been analysing the wool types, to detect forty-seven different yarns and stitching threads and one unspun staple, and he was able to show that the majority were of a hairy type such as could be readily obtained from northern British sheep. Dr John Peter Wild's initial studies of the weaving patterns indicate that all the standard Roman weaves are represented in the Vindolanda textiles. There is nothing which could not have been made in the north of Britain. Several fragments include selvedges and stitching, and many examples of woollen girdles in plain weave, some 2–2¼ inches wide, were found which could have been worn by both men and women, knotted in the front rather than fastened with a belt-buckle. There are also, however, fragments of plain two-over-two twill, of good tweed-suiting quality, half-basket weave, two-over-two diamond-twill weave, fine diamond twills and an unusual 'hairy' plain weave. Some fragments of felt, such as would have provided a lining for helmets and similar gear, were discovered too.

Plates 67–69, XIV

To the naked eye, all the cloth (with one exception) appeared to be the same dull yellowish-brown colour, but microscopic examination showed Dr Wild that the half-basket weave fabric had a broad purple stripe across it, tapestry woven, as did the piece from the Walbrook site in London. This was an exciting discovery, because at that date (no later than AD 110) the purple stripe or *clavus* was the distinctive badge of rank of the Roman aristocracy, and the only man likely to qualify for this at Vindolanda would have been the regiment's commanding officer. Like the writing tablets, this piece must have come across from another building in a pile of rubbish.

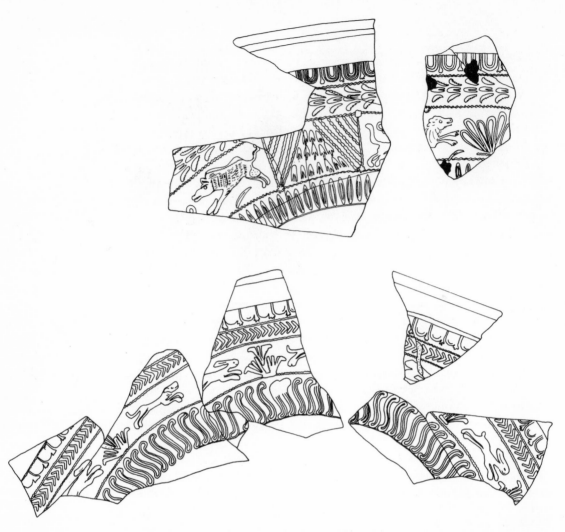

39, 40 Fragments of two Samian bowls, the more expensive tableware made in South Gaul in the late first century

One other large fragment had a checked pattern in parallel vertical bands, visible to the naked eye, and it may represent the remains of a bed cover or similar article.

There were some surprises in the collection, which may ultimately prove to have been caused by the accidents of chance discovery. No linen or silk was found although both should survive in these soils, but the area examined was small in relation to the whole deposit and future work may correct the balance. We hope, too, to find more evidence for weaving: a weaving frame, for example, would be more substantial proof than the few combs unearthed so far. Anthony Hedley's old cottage at Chesterholm was constructed in 1831 on the site of an old fulling mill, and fuller's earth is reported to be in good supply locally. The Romans, on the other hand, may have used the alternative ingredient for fulling – well-decayed urine – which would also have been in good supply, at the outlets to the fort's latrines.

Pottery

The pottery from the early deposits (some 500 different rim fragments) can be securely dated to the period before Vindolanda was temporarily abandoned on the construction of the Hadrianic Wall forts. Samian ware was predominantly of South Gaulish origin, although the Central Gaulish factories were making some inroads into the market in periods III and IV. The coarse pottery included the typical roughcast and rustic wares, and the sandy yellowish *mortaria*: the dominant type was the carinated bowl with flat or reeded rim, largely in buff and orange fabrics, which never reappeared on the reoccupation of the site after the middle of the second century. Black-burnished ware (BBI) also appeared in the III and IV levels, although in very small quantities. Earlier survivals were represented by a fragment of Belgic ware, with stamp, from the period I rampart.

A high proportion of this early pottery carried scratched or painted graffiti, and the decline in literacy on the frontier can be gauged by the increasing rarity of graffiti as time went by. Many of the scrawls were the work of men who wished to remind others that a pot was their property,

Figs. 39, 40

Plate 70

Fig. 41

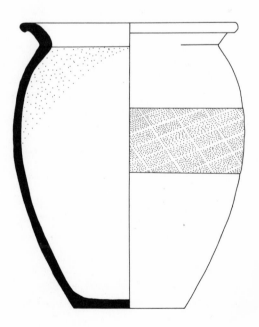

41 *Black-burnished ware, such as this cooking pot, appeared in small quantities in the pre-Hadrianic periods III and IV deposits*

Plate 71

and it would not be surprising to discover that army regulations insisted upon such markings. There were two particularly fine graffiti amongst the batch from the period II floor: one, painted on the neck of an amphora, records the contents of the jar as 'prime mackerel sauce', the product perhaps of Lusitania;[119] the other, boldly incised on the shoulder of a dark-grey flagon, recorded the weight of the vessel as $8\frac{1}{2}$ Roman pounds (just over 6 pounds, or 2.8 kilograms), and the full weight as 30 (or more) pounds.

Coins and other small finds

Coins were few and far between: only five were recovered from periods II and III and none from periods I and IV. All were bronze *sestertii* of Domitian and Trajan, thus providing support for the dating of the occupation suggested by the pottery and the dated writing tablet.

Plate 26

There was a scatter of the sort of small finds which one might expect inside any fort, and they were notable here only because of their unusually fine state of preservation. Bronze items still shone like gold, and the ironwork was uncorroded. Iron items included ballista bolts, a sickle, two heavy stone-hammers (one of which, inscribed with the name of the centurion, weighed 14 pounds 8 ounces), knives, needles, four keys (two of which still had the leather thongs through the holes in the handles), thirteen stylus pens, a razor, meat hooks, a variety of objects of unknown use, and a

Plate 72

multitude of nails, ranging from small studs to others which put the modern 6-inch nail to shame. Bronzes were not as plentiful, but the group contained two trumpet brooches in working order, three *spatulae*, an ear-

Plate 73

ring pendant, a larger pendant and numerous scraps of bronze strip lining (of the sort found on shields). Other items included numerous wooden barrel-staves and bungs, a bone scraper and the inevitable bone gaming-

Plate 74

pieces. From the 1974 section, we were able to add a fine bone dice to this collection, although it proved to be a speciality piece, heavily loaded in favour of the numbers six and one.

Environmental evidence

The information which we can obtain from the organic remains is as important as much of the artifactual evidence. Amongst the most significant of the preliminary observations made by Dr Mark Seaward is the discovery that bracken harvesting was a major, time-consuming occupation. One small room excavated in 1973, approximately 16 feet by 12 feet, contained enough bracken to require a crop of $2\frac{1}{2}$ acres. Admittedly, this carpet had been laid over a period of years – perhaps as many as five or six years – but bracken floors were the norm in period II and remained an important ingredient in periods III and IV, so that the total harvest necessary for the needs of the fort must have required weeks of work by the majority of the men. Bracken is still plentiful on the slopes of Barcombe Hill near the site, and some neighbouring farmers harvested the crop until very recently, using it as winter bedding for cattle. At Vindolanda, there is evidence to suggest that the bracken had been stored for some time before use, and there were thus few traces of the insects normally associated with bracken.

Remains of wood were plentiful, and analysis of a representative group[120] revealed that birch, oak, hazel and ash were predominant, with a few rowan, yew, pine and cherry. Wooden objects were most frequently made of oak and ash, but the building posts were normally taken from the ubiquitous birch tree. Macrophytic remains included hazel-nuts, walnuts, acorns, gorse-pods and heather stems. Particular attention in the future will focus upon the evidence for the growing of cereal crops, to test the theory that the Romans destroyed most of the existing native cereals and relied upon imported corn from the south of England.

VIII   The writing tablets

Discovery and excavation

The discovery of the writing tablets transformed the excavation. The state of preservation of the organic material in the pre-Hadrianic layers was remarkable enough to give us an insight into Roman living conditions which we could never have anticipated, and the textiles were particularly welcome. But if Roman documents could survive – and every Roman archaeologist has looked with envy upon the great finds of the past, such as the papyrus records from the fort at Dura-Europos on the Euphrates[121] – then the archaeological horizons would be extended to lengths undreamed of in Britain. What was more, the super-imposed timber buildings offered precise dating – precise in the relatively loose archaeological sense – for the layers had been deposited between AD 80 (at the very earliest, and perhaps only just pre-AD 90) and AD 125, when the pottery and epigraphic evidence fully supported the historical inference that the garrison moved up to a new Wall fort, probably at Housesteads.

If I have to spend the rest of my life working in dirty, wet trenches, I doubt whether I shall ever again experience the shock and excitement I felt at my first glimpse of ink hieroglyphics on tiny scraps of wood. In the middle of March 1973 the three permanent staff had devoted some time to removing the in-fill from the previous autumn's drainage trench and bottoming the deposit (see chapter VI). There was a great deal of wood amongst the straw and bracken, ranging from oak beams and planking to wattle-fencing and twigs. While trowelling this deposit I came across two small thin fragments of wood, which looked rather like oily plane shavings. I wondered if this was evidence for wood-working on the spot, and passed one fragment up to my assistant on the surface for his opinion. He examined the wood and passed it back to me, observing that it seemed to have some peculiar marks on it. I had another look and thought I must have been dreaming, for the marks appeared to be ink writing. We took the piece over to the excavation hut and gently cleaned it, discovering that there were in fact two slivers of wood adhering to each other. After gently prizing them apart with a knife, we stared at the tiny writing in utter disbelief. Within four hours, still shaken, we were sitting in the drawing-room of an eminent epigraphist, Mr Richard Wright, in Durham, awaiting his verdict and opinion on what to do with the evidence. Fortunately, his experience and advice ensured that the wood was taken to the Department of Photography at Newcastle University for detailed photography – and the long process of research began.

The first large group of tablets (whose distribution can be seen on the plan) was found in the period II floor (*c.* AD 95–105); subsequently, however, tablets were discovered in all four occupation deposits. The general state of these floors has already been described. In relation to the *vicus*, the tablets lay below the most southerly structures excavated in 1959[122] just off the south-west angle of the later stone fort. It is more difficult to determine their position in relation to the various pre-Hadrianic forts. The 5 tablets from period I (pre-AD 90) came from the ditch of that fort, outside its south-east angle, but those from the period II fort (the great majority: 171) came from a structure part of which was probably being used as a *fabrica* or workshop, although whether this was the regimental workshop or a smaller structure attached to another building such as the commanding officer's residence is not yet clear. The tablets from the periods III and IV floors, few in number and mostly fragmentary, belong to a building of unknown use.

Fig. 30

The tablets can be divided into three types. First of all there are the stylus-tablets, recessed pieces of wood which were once coated with wax so that messages could be incised upon them with a metal stylus. The incisions made in the wood as the stylus cut through the wax are still clearly visible on certain of the 14 such tablets unearthed. Most of them are from the period III and IV deposits. Secondly there is a single example of a stylus-tablet which has been written upon in ink rather than incised. This may or may not be contemporary with the other tablets, since it was found in the fourth-century Diocletianic ditch which cut through and disturbed the pre-Hadrianic material. The great majority of the tablets, however, can be classed in the third category, the ink writing tablets, only one of which had ever been found in Britain before.[123] These are flat, thin slices of limewood, made to carry writing in ink on one or both surfaces. Many are wafer-thin – often less than $\frac{1}{16}$ inch thick – and the only complete examples measure at most $4\frac{3}{4}$ inches by $1\frac{2}{3}$ inches. Their excavation caused considerable problems. They were so fragile that the smallest pressure – such as occurred when a bracken frond was accidentally moved – was liable to cause fractures, and most of them were effectively glued to the surrounding organic rubbish. Trowelling the floors was thus fatal for the tablets, as it was for much of the organic material and for the textiles, and experience soon demonstrated that the only effective way of extracting them was to cut the flooring in the manner of peat, and then, in good light

Plate 75

Plates 76–82, XIII

out of the trench, carefully peel the layers apart on the natural break lines. In this way tablets could be located and extracted, usually on a small piece of organic matter, without any handling at all.

Preservation

Once the fragments had been recovered the immediate problem was to evolve some method of preserving them. In most cases no writing was visible to the naked eye, although where two or more (up to a maximum of five) leaves were stuck together, the ink was clearly visible on the inner sheets for about a quarter of an hour after they were peeled apart. Infra-red photography proved to be the salvation, but first the tablets had to be cleaned. This was carried out on the site in the laboratory, and it took many hours of painstaking and nerve-wracking concentration. The tablets arrived from the trenches in polythene self-sealing bags, with the find-spot written on the bag. They were taken out and placed in saucers of water, and left to soak for up to five days. Then, with a blunt knife – a scalpel was too liable to scrape away the vital surface – and fine brushes, the adhering dirt was gently removed. The most difficult part of the process lay in separating conjoining leaves, especially those of the five-leaf tablet no. 90 which was much battered and fractured, but the excitement of opening the leaves, after hours of cleaning, to see line upon line of minute writing is beyond description.

Once cleaning was completed, the tablets were packed into polythene boxes, soaked in water and a disinfectant and taken to the Department of Photography at Newcastle University. It is worth stressing at this point that however much care is taken by the excavators, the real dangers for the tablets lie outside the trenches. At least six people have to handle them at various times, and they need to remain for days and sometimes weeks in laboratories, where the curious but careless visitor can unwittingly cause irreparable damage. It is a great credit to all concerned that only two small scraps of one tablet were lost during the processing.

Plates 76, 77

At Newcastle University, Miss Alison Rutherford photographed the tablets under three conditions – normal light, ultra-violet and infra-red. Infra-red photography soon became the standard method, however, when it was discovered by Miss Rutherford that carbon-based ink, which shows up particularly well on this type of film, was the ink used on the Vindolanda tablets. She produced the first prints for both site laboratory and the specialists who had undertaken to study them (see below). The tablets then went to the Research Laboratory at the British Museum, where Mr W. A. Oddy and Mrs Susan Blackshaw shouldered the burden of treating them, under the supervision of Dr A. E. A. Werner. The development here of a successful method of preservation was a major break-through, and the loss through shrinkage was rarely more than 3 per cent. In many cases ink writing was now visible to the naked eye on tablets which had appeared to be blank, and a further round of photography at Newcastle confirmed that the ink was easier to see, so that the specialists had much less difficulty with the second series of photographs. Recently an American technique which combines ultra-violet with infra-red photography has been attempted by Miss Rutherford with considerable success on some of the tablets, but its use is still in the experimental stage.

The problems of decipherment

At this stage, all that had been achieved after many months of work by a host of people was a series of photographs showing tiny spidery scrawls, which to the uninitiated were written in some unknown language. Eminent Latin epigraphists, familiar with the complexities of stone inscriptions, which employed a capital script much like that in use today, were baffled by the cursive writing on the tablets. This latter script was probably the one most commonly used in Roman times, and as such tended to be written more quickly and less legibly than the capital form. Through the good offices of Mr Richard Wright and Professor Barri Jones we were therefore fortunate to secure the services of two of the few specialists in Britain who could read such material, Dr David Thomas of Durham University and Dr Alan Bowman of Manchester University. Richard Wright, himself one of the leading epigraphists in Britain, was deeply involved in the interpretation of the texts in the initial stages, but gradually the main burden fell upon Drs Bowman and Thomas, whose experience with papyri gave them advantages denied to the epigraphist.[124]

Even if one has great experience of ancient cursive writing, the task of decipherment is still long and complicated. Few tablets are complete and few are without patches of faded ink or awkward grains in the wood. The worst problem, however, is that several of the letters have been drawn in such a way as to appear virtually indistinguishable to the modern eye from certain other letters. Thus, for example, on some texts an 'a' and an 'r', an 'e' and an 's' or a 'c' and a 'p' are almost identical. Bowman and Thomas have detected over forty different hands so far, and each writer had his own peculiarities. There are few capital letters, many abbreviations, no punctuation and much phonetic spelling. Nevertheless, despite these difficulties, many of the tablets have now been successfully deciphered and their content revealed.

The content of the tablets

Bowman and Thomas discovered that several of the 202 tablets were blank, which may imply that they had never been used: the fragile nature of the thin sheets of wood indicates that many must have been accidentally broken before use and discarded. It is possible, however, that some were written on in an ink which does not respond to either infra-red or ultra-violet photography. A variety of secret inks were employed in the Roman period, ranging from fresh milk (which became visible when charcoal dust was sprinkled over it) to linseed oil, but it is doubtful whether we will ever be able to read such writing now.[125] Many of the tablets with visible writing were fragmentary, and some bore traces of burning as though dead files had been partially destroyed at one time; these damaged pieces often yielded only a few words or letters. All the fragments are nonetheless valuable to the palaeographer and the linguist.

The more complete examples so far deciphered fall into two broad categories: accounts and private correspondence. All relate to the regiment in garrison at Vindolanda before Hadrian's Wall was constructed, which may have been the First Cohort of Tungrians (see chapter VI), the later garrison of Housesteads on the Wall. In this connection it is interesting to note that the one official as opposed to private letter discovered to date should be addressed to the commanding officer, reporting the safe arrival at York of a detachment of Tungrians. Unfortunately this document has not yet been fully deciphered.

Private correspondence

One tablet (no. 31) from the period II deposit, made up of two fragments comprising a single leaf, seems to have been the draft rather than the final copy of a letter, because, unusually, the text was written on both sides of the wood and an above-average number of lines had been crossed out or amended. This would help to explain the curious fact revealed by part of the text that the letter was sent from not to Vindolanda (which is named). The twenty-six lines of writing, addressed to a certain Crispinus, are full of commonplaces about the conditions of military service. In the second half of the letter, however, a man named L. Neratius Marcellus is mentioned, who is known from an inscription found elsewhere to have been the governor of Britain between AD 101 and 103. Marcellus was a friend or acquaintance of Pliny the Younger (*c.* AD 61/2–114), the celebrated senator and man of letters, and thus here in a single reference the tablets give us the kind of glimpse into the classical literary and historical worlds that ordinary archaeological data so rarely afford. But quite apart from its intrinsic interest this new information provides an invaluable means of checking the

42 Some finds recovered from the late fort's ditch. Top row, left to right: part of a bronze bridle-bit, bronze bureau handle and wooden comb; middle row: polished bone ornament, seal box and shale lathe-end; bottom row: series of iron links, bone fan holder (?), and a palette for mixing cosmetics.

43 A rare bronze zoomorphic brooch (seen in plate 44, top row, second from left) which may once have been the property of a late-fourth-century Theodosian mercenary.

44 Bronze brooches of various kinds from the civilian settlement.

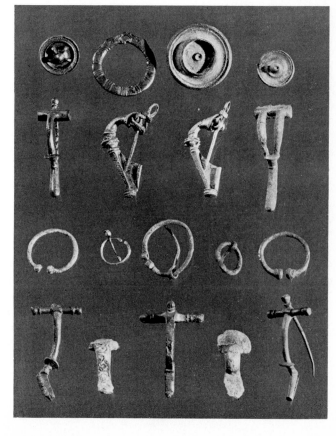

45   A selection of silver coins from the civilian settlement.

46, 47   The jet betrothal medallion (shown also in colour plate VI) from the alleyway east of the *mansio*. The obverse (*left*) portrays a man and woman apparently kissing – the woman's hair-style indicates a date in the last quarter of the third century A D. The clasped hands on the reverse (*right*) symbolize the signing of a bond, no doubt in this case the marriage bond. The medallion was probably made near York, from Whitby jet.

48, 49 Excavations within the stone fort in 1934. (*Above*) The administrative rooms in the headquarters building, showing the hypocaust system introduced in the final phase of occupation (after A D 367). (*Below*) Traces of the strange circular buildings (subsequently back–filled) underlying the north wall of the fort, to the east of the north gate. (Scales in feet.)

50 Ornamental screen from the administrative rooms in the late headquarters building, re-erected (in the wrong place) by the Department of the Environment. (Scale in feet.)

51 The north-east corner of the fort wall, excavated in 1972, showing the twin sewer exits (immediately to the right of the ranging pole; scale in feet).

52, 53 Excavations within the pre-Hadrianic wooden forts. (*Above*) Part of the period IIa floor, showing the *fabrica* or workshop. The large posts on the left and in the trench edge belong to a later structure. (*Below*) The remains of the eastern wattle walls of the period IIa/IIb structure, effectively demolished by Roman soldiers. (Scales in feet.)

54, 55 Pre-Hadrianic timber structures. (*Above*) Timber wall foundations of a period IIIa building, with major uprights morticed into short lengths of sleeper beam. (*Below*) A sill-beam-like structure on the floor of the *fabrica*, period IIa. (Scales in feet.)

56, 57 The timber gate found outside the *fabrica*; it had been deliberately placed in position on a raised stone platform, and may have served as the base for a water tank connected with leather tanning. (*Above*) The gate as it was discovered, 7 feet below the roadway of *c.* AD 300. (*Below*) The frame of the gate after the planking had been removed. (Scales in feet.)

58, 59   Animal skulls from the pre-Hadrianic forts. (*Above*) Three skulls of Roman oxen; the one on the left has been used for target practice. (*Below*) The skull of a nine-year-old gelding, flanked by red-deer antlers and the skulls of a goat and sheep.

60 Wooden combs and bone implements from the pre-Hadrianic forts. The combs had apparently been used for de-hairing hides.

61, 62 (*Left*) One of the tens of thousands of stable-fly pupae found preserved in the bracken flooring of the *fabrica* (period IIa). (*Right*) Many of the pupae contained the fully formed bodies of the flies, and in this magnified (× 500) example, one can see details of the insect's leg.

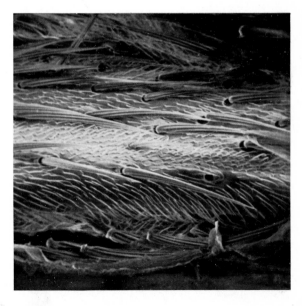

63, 64 Leatherwork from the pre-Hadrianic deposits. (*Above*) A leather bag with patches above it and fragmentary thongs on either side. (*Below*) Most of the shoes found had been stripped of their uppers – like these – and in some cases the nails had been withdrawn for re-use (e.g. the example on the left).

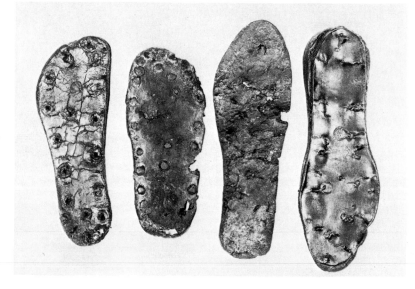

65, 66 Ladies' leather footwear from the pre-Hadrianic deposits. (*Below left*) A shoe, 9¾ inches long. (*Below right*) The lady's 'Persian' slipper stamped with the letters L. AEB. THALES T. F., which presumably stands for 'Lucius Aebutius Thales, son of Titus', the name of the maker of the shoe. Other stamps portray a vine leaf and *cornucopiae*, symbols of fertility.

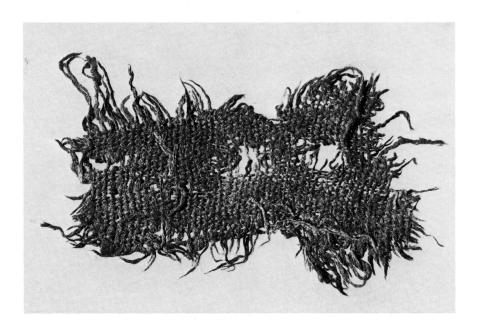

67–69 Three contrasting types of woollen textile, between $5\frac{1}{2}$ and $6\frac{1}{2}$ inches long, from the pre-Hadrianic deposits.

70, 71   Pre-Hadrianic pottery. (*Above*) A two-handled flagon, big enough to hold 2 litres of wine, stands at the back next to a typical early bowl with reeded rim; in front are a richly decorated Samian bowl from South Gaul, a small votive lamp and a large mixing bowl or *mortaria*, with the maker's name stamped on the rim. (*Below*) Fragment of a storage vessel, with a graffito recording the weight of the vessel as 8½ Roman pounds (just over 6 pounds) and the weight when full as 30 (or more) pounds.

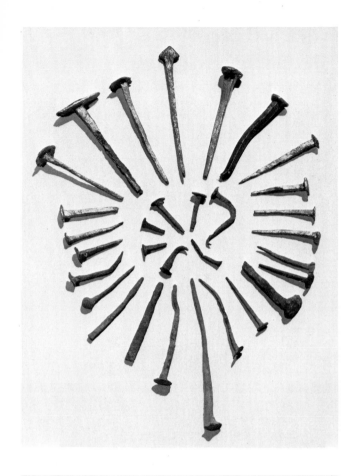

72 A selection of nails from the pre-Hadrianic forts, ranging from small tacks to 4-inch brads.

73 A bronze earring pendant from the floor of the *fabrica* (period IIa) in the pre-Hadrianic fort.

74 A stone gaming board, with counters, dice box and dice. The latter, from the pre-Hadrianic fort, proved to be heavily loaded in favour of the numbers six and one.

75 A complete stylus tablet (no. 123) from the 1974 excavations in the pre-Hadrianic deposits. On this example there is no trace of writing.

76, 77 Writing tablet no. 15 photographed on ordinary film (*left*) and infra-red film (*right*). The two leaves were found folded together; when opened the writing was still visible to the naked eye, but it gradually faded on exposure to the air. The text is part of a private letter and lists various garments – sandals, socks and underpants – which were being sent to the recipient at Vindolanda.

78 Infra-red photograph of tablet no. 129, found in the period IV pre-Hadrianic floor in 1974. The letter is addressed on the outside to a private soldier, a decurion named Lucius, and records the receipt of a gift of forty oysters.

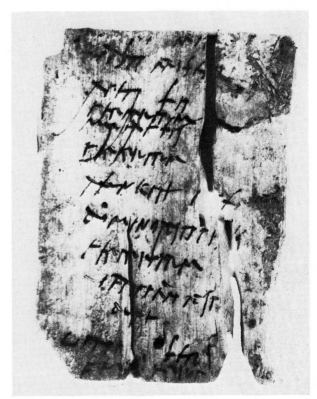

79, 80   Two leaves from the multi-leaved official stores inventory (no. 33), which records the dispensation of food-stuffs, predominantly meat, over a period of eight days in June in a year unspecified. The leaves would have been bound together through the tie-holes visible at the top (*left*) and bottom (*right*), a 'concertina' format so far otherwise unknown from classical antiquity.

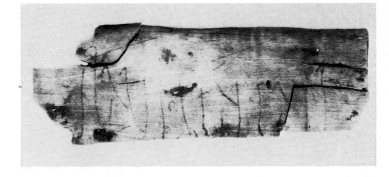

81   A typical example, yet to be deciphered, of a scrawled address found on many of the ink tablets.

82   A fragmentary tablet (no. 39) from the pre-Hadrianic period IIa – *fabrica* – floor, exhibiting an elegant form of handwriting.

83 The replica stone and turf walls under construction. The simulated Roman scaffolding had later to be removed to comply with modern safety standards.

84 The timber milecastle gateway set into the turf wall, and constructed by staff and pupils from Gateshead Schools.

dating of period II, which on archaeological grounds falls within the years AD 95–105. Although we cannot be certain how old the letter was when it was thrown away, the combined weight of literary and archaeological evidence now make it unlikely that the deposit was laid down after AD 105.

The remaining letters consist of incoming mail, in a variety of hands and for a variety of people. One (no. 29), of which two sections survive, was addressed on the outside to a man called Cerialis, almost certainly the commanding officer of Vindolanda at the time. Bowman and Thomas have translated the first part of the incomplete text, crudely scrawled on the inner faces of the two tablets, as follows:[126] '[Name] is my dear friend and a capable fellow. He has requested me, my lord, to recommend him to you. I therefore ask you, my lord, that whatever he may request of you, you will agree to let him have.' The letter concludes: 'thus through helping him you will have put me under an obligation to you as your debtor'. A separate hand has added, at the bottom of the letter, 'Farewell, brother': this was probably inserted by the actual sender, no doubt a man of rank who could afford to use a scribe for the remainder. Such letters of recommendation were a common feature of Roman life, and nowhere more so than in the army: our letter will have been intended to help advance the career of a new recruit, perhaps a young subaltern who had just joined the Vindolanda garrison.

Another letter (no. 15) is also represented by two sections with writing on the inner faces, but here there is no address on the outside and what survives is a smaller fraction of the complete letter. The first part of the text, in a competent hand, mentions two pairs of sandals, an unspecified number of woollen socks and two pairs of underpants (*subligaria*), all of which are being sent to the recipient at Vindolanda. The second incomplete section contains the concluding part of the letter, in which the writer sends greetings to various named individuals (Elpis – a Greek name meaning 'Hope' – and Tetricus are the only decipherable ones) as well as to 'all your messmates; I pray that you and they may enjoy long life and the best of fortune'. Despite the seemingly mundane nature of the letter, it provides important information regarding soldiers' clothing on the northern frontier *c.* AD 100. Common sense has always suggested that soldiers would have worn socks and underpants in cooler climates, at least in winter, but because these articles are rarely represented on Roman monuments (Trajan's Column does not record them) the matter has been open to argument. Now the Vindolanda tablets have confirmed that, even if socks and underpants were not part of the soldier's regular uniform, they were at least worn occasionally as additional clothing.

Letter no. 129, addressed on the outside to a decurion named Lucius, contains similarly commonplace information which yet serves to support

Plate XIII

Plates 76, 77

Plate 78

an inference drawn from purely archaeological evidence. The writer asks after the recipient's health, and goes on to remark that 'A friend has sent me forty oysters from Cordonovi [?]'. We know from the excavations that oysters and mussels were part of the diet – as they were on many Roman sites; the letter could suggest that they were a luxury rather than a staple for the Roman gourmet, since they were valued enough to be sent as a gift to the writer.

Official accounts

Besides private correspondence there are also several fragmentary tablets which contain accounts relating to the military organization at the fort. The most important group has been published by Dr Bowman.[127]

Plates 79, 80

He pointed out that five large leaves, two medium-sized fragments and ten small fragments, found at different times (inventory nos. 33, 47 and 62), belong to one document comprising forty-five short lines of writing. Study of the internal evidence of the texts, the adhesion of some of the pieces to each other and the external physical features of the leaves (including the position of tie-holes) led him to postulate a 'concertina' format so far otherwise unknown from classical antiquity. The diagram

Fig. 42

illustrates the suggested original form of the document. The bottom of leaf *b* would have been joined to the top of *c* through the tie-holes, and *d* to *e* likewise, while *a* and *b* (and *c* and *d* also) would have formed one 'double-page', as it were, scored down the middle to fold, not cut in two. Thus when the document was opened, simply by holding the top leaf (*a*) and pulling the bottom leaf (*e*), the text would have unfolded into a single continuous column which could have been read from top to bottom. Dr Bowman has pointed out that this exciting discovery may represent an intermediate stage between the roll (as in papyrus), with its long continuous columns, and the codex, with its separate leaves. The fact that we have no other such example from classical antiquity is probably due only to lack of research.

The surviving fragments of the document refer to payments and supplies over a period of eight days in the month of June, in a year unspecified. The first few lines record deposits of money or payments made *ad sacrum*, which may mean payments into the regimental strong-room (*sacellum*) or alternatively money set aside for sacrificial or religious purposes. The main part of the document, however, comprises a list of foodstuffs, with a quantity stated afterwards. This list, together with that from a separate, smaller account (no. 11, another 'concertina'-format document with about twenty lines of writing), gives an excellent picture of the diet of Roman soldiers at the very beginning of the second century. The most frequently mentioned item is barley (*hordeum*), whereas other cereals such as corn

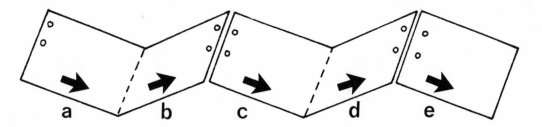

42 *Diagram illustrating the original form of the multi-leaved official stores inventory (nos. 33, 47 and 62), as proposed by Dr Alan Bowman. The leaves would have been joined through the tie-holes marked; the whole document could then have been read from top to bottom as indicated by the arrows*

(*frumentum*) – normally regarded as a staple item – and malting corn (*bracis*) are referred to only once each. The appearance of so much barley is surprising since the crop was normally used as animal fodder, but Dr Bowman points out that by June, the month to which the larger account with all the barley entries refers, the troops may have had to eat it due to a shortage of wheat. The lists also include fish sauce (*muria*) – perhaps the mackerel sauce specified on the amphora found in 1973 (see p. 130) – pork fat (*axungia*), spices (*condimenta*), salt (*sal*), vintage wine (*vinum*), sour wine (*acetum*, the soldier's ordinary drink), Celtic beer (*cervesa*, in very small quantities compared with the wine), goat's meat (*caprea*), young pig (*porcellum*), ham (*perna*) and venison (*cervina*). These latter items, taken in conjunction with the thousands of food-bones found on the floors of the buildings, provide overwhelming evidence to disprove the theory held until recently that Roman soldiers ate little meat.[128] But whether the troops were given such a variety of meat as a regular part of their rations it is impossible to say, since the account with a majority of the meat entries (no. 11) may relate to some special festive occasion, such as a dinner for the *Saturnalia*. The other account (nos. 33, 47, and 62) states specifically in four places that the commodities were for private use (*per privatum*), suggesting that they were being issued over and above regular rations.

Quite apart from the detailed information these accounts give us about Roman military diet, they demonstrate how closely monitored were all aspects of life in the army. Supervisors and clerks kept a watchful eye on the storage and issue of supplies, recording even mundane transactions.

The importance of the tablets

The importance of the tablets cannot be over-stressed. To begin with, they have thrown new light on a phase in the history of the northern frontier

155

which is not well served by evidence of any kind. This period, between the recall of the governor Agricola and Hadrian's visit to Britain (AD 85–122), is one of great significance: Agricola departed for Italy with the Roman army apparently victorious and encamped in the foothills of the Scottish Highlands; Hadrian arrived to inspect the construction of his Wall between Tyne and Solway, far to the south of Agricola's forward line. Yet the accidents of survival have denied to us any literary evidence for this period, and the few inscriptions extant, although valuable, do not allow us to construct a meaningful history. The first group of tablets from Vindolanda to be deciphered, securely dated to within a few years of AD 100, has already shown that the information the documents provide can range from the names of the governors of Britain, to knowledge of troop movements and the soldiers' clothing, diet and conditions of service in the north. Future research will undoubtedly broaden this list.

The tablets are also of major importance to the study of ancient Latin. They are written in a kind of Vulgar Latin which is relatively unfamiliar to us, since the surviving literary works of classical authors mostly employ a more refined tongue. Now we have the opportunity to learn something of the colloquial Latin used by the man in the street. Already, for example, several spellings have been found to differ from those used by literary authors, such as *annuas* for *adnuas*, *debetor* for *debitor* and *karus* for *carus*. These probably represent phonetic spellings, that is, attempts by the scribes to write down the words as they sounded. In this way we gain an insight into how ancient Latin was spoken, an area of our knowledge that was previously very thin.

Besides linguists, palaeographers – students of ancient writing – have also recognized the great value of the Vindolanda documents. Hitherto our understanding of Latin script in the first two centuries AD has had to depend very largely upon papyri from Egypt. The discovery of written material from the opposite, northern end of the empire therefore neatly balances the Egyptian evidence. Moreover the Vindolanda tablets are not only securely dated, they are also written in over forty different hands, which provide the palaeographer with a remarkable diversity of styles to analyse: some of the scripts are crude, a majority merely competent, while one or two approach the level of calligraphy. Although it will be many years before the British and Egyptian material has been thoroughly compared, preliminary study indicates that the scripts from the two areas are surprisingly similar.

Plate 81
Plate 82

It is quite certain that many more tablets still lie buried beneath the civilian buildings at Vindolanda, waiting to be excavated. Indeed the documents may eventually be numbered in thousands not hundreds. Besides the letters and stores–lists already found there could be pay-sheets, requisition forms, daily orders, the annual regimental stock-taking of both men and supplies, confidential career records and all kinds of other material relating to the Roman army and administration. Looking farther afield, there is no reason why similar evidence should not be discovered on some of the other sites in the north of England where equally good soil conditions obtain. But in the meantime, while the money and the men are raised to test these hypotheses, we should look with wonder on the remarkable finds that have already been made since that first chance discovery of the pre-Hadrianic deposits during ditch-digging in 1972.

IX   Replica construction

Planning and initiation of the project

The construction of full-scale replicas of ancient buildings is a subject upon which many people have decided views. For several years there have been those who have felt that a reconstructed length of Hadrian's Wall, upon the Whin Sill crags and perhaps by Housesteads milecastle, would serve as a stimulating experiment of great archaeological and educational value which would also enhance the appeal of the ruins nearby. Nothing was done to implement this scheme, however, mainly because of lack of support from the government authorities concerned. It was not until the foundation of the Vindolanda Trust in 1970 that the opportunity for replica construction arose.

At Vindolanda a small area of marshy land in the south-western corner of the field appeared to lie outside the limits of the settlement and clear of the cemeteries (although, as we later discovered, only just clear of a late burial ground). With the expansion of the Trust's educational activities and the increasing weight of schools visits, it seemed appropriate that the first attempt to construct a replica should be made on this piece of land. It would have been more satisfactory to build closer to the Wall, but at least Vindolanda counted as a Wall fort from the mid-second century and the majority of our visitors would be familiar with the low-standing remains to the north.

I devised a possible scheme in the spring of 1972 and placed it before the Trustees. The proposal was for a 25-yard section of wall in turf, copying as closely as possible the Turf Wall, or length of Hadrian's Wall west of the river Irthing which was eventually rebuilt in stone in the late second century. Following the known specifications of the stretch examined west of Birdoswald fort, our turf wall was to be 25 feet wide at base, rising to a rampart walk 15 feet high with a 6-foot timber palisade on the forward edge. Joining this wall at right-angles (due to lack of space) would be a stone wall, 15 yards long, 10 feet wide at base, 15 feet high to the rampart walk and with a 6-feet-high and 2-feet-thick crenellated parapet. These were roughly the dimensions of the Broad Wall, the name given to the first plan for Hadrian's Wall before the builders reduced the width to a less imposing but more economical 8 feet, the Narrow Wall, after *c.* AD 125.[129]

Fig. 44

Fig. 45

Both turf and stone walls were to have their regulation ditches on the outer side, 30 feet wide and at least 10 feet deep.

A majority of the Trustees approved the plan and we began work in earnest. The first problem to overcome was that of manpower. Our regular number of volunteers was capable of constructing the stone wall under the watchful eye and with the skilled assistance of the Trust's own mason, Mr Jimmy Biggs, but the turf wall required larger forces. Accordingly I wrote to Mr Les Turnbull, then senior history master at Heathfield Senior High School in Gateshead, asking if we might enlist his help. He accepted at once – like myself, perhaps not quite appreciating the consequences at the time – and together with colleagues and pupils from his school has provided the main workforce for the entire turf wall project.

Our second problem was that of finance. Even though 90 per cent of the labour was free, the total bill eventually came to about £5,000, of which over £1,000 was for timber. This was much less than the £25,000 which a local building firm estimated would have been the true cost, including labour, but nevertheless it was an impossibly large sum for the Vindolanda Trust to cope with. We were very fortunate, therefore, to receive generous support from the Gateshead Education Committee, Mr Alex Cussons and the English Tourist Board.

Quite apart from the difficulties we faced in starting the project, there were enormous problems of construction to be solved. The original builders of Hadrian's Wall had been confronted by these too: the 70-mile length of Wall traversed terrain as varied as the shifting sands on the Solway, the steep but uneven crags of the Whin Sill and the gentle slopes leading down to the Tyne, none of which afforded flat platforms for construction. Undoubtedly there would have been a blueprint with standard measurements marked on it, but the actual builders must have had to adapt this plan to suit the nature of the ground. Hence, for example the regulation height and width of the Wall cannot have been strictly observed on gradients, otherwise the rampart walk would have been nothing but a series of steep steps. By the same token, level foundation platforms must have been constructed first for the many stretches of wall which were erected on ground sloping sharply in two directions. It was the similarity of these problems to the ones we faced in replica construction at Vindolanda that made our research so valuable.

We did not intend to keep a detailed record of the man-hours spent by the labour gangs since the quality of the volunteers varied so much. Nor did we think it worthwhile to use imitation Roman tools, or an ox-wagon instead of a tractor and trailer; there were limits, usually financial, to the extent to which we could copy Roman methods. But we did keep accurate records of the quantities of the different materials used, and we conducted

Fig. 43

Plate 83

elementary time-and-motion studies on particular aspects of the work. The information we eventually gained exceeded our most optimistic forecasts.

The turf wall

Fig. 44

In the Doe Sike field the site of the turf wall was such that the ground sloped downwards a distance of 3 feet from the proposed back to the proposed front of the structure. The ground also descended from the west to the east end a further 5 feet. Thus, from the highest corner diagonally across to the lowest, there was a fall of 8 feet. The foundations, therefore, had to be stepped in two directions to obviate the risk of movement forward and along the line of the wall. To excavate a level platform would have been an enormous task, but the problem was overcome by levelling the front half of the site and removing the steep gradient. The result of this arrangement was that in the 25 yards of the turf wall, the height of the completed rampart walk from the ground varied between 12 feet and 17 feet.

When it became necessary to design the rampart walk, there was no archaeological evidence to show what the arrangement had once been. But illustrations of ramparts with crenellations on Trajan's Column, together with representations of Hadrian's Wall on the Rudge Cup and the Amiens Skillet (and common sense, too), suggested that Hadrian's Wall did have a crenellated rampart. In the absence of any hard details pure guesswork had to be employed, based on certain principles. The structure had to be secure enough to withstand strong wind pressure against the rampart face; it must be impressive, to conform with the general appearance of the frontier; and the design must be simple to construct and economical in materials.

Ian Richmond's published reconstruction drawings[130] show the timber parapet resting neatly on top of the Turf Wall, but our joiners considered such a form of construction structurally weak, impractical to build, unimpressive to look at and too expensive in timber. In particular it was doubted whether such a rampart would withstand the impact of a southerly gale. More complicated plans had to be drawn up. Our rampart came to consist of wooden boarding fixed to upright posts which were positioned at the ends of each merlon. The spacing of the merlons and their size was purely conjectural. The rampart was secured below the turf walk by a triangular arrangement of timbers formed by the lower 6 feet of the upright, a sleeper beam and a diagonal brace. Each pair of uprights was fastened to the adjacent pair on both sides by horizontal braces fixed to the sleeper beams and the uprights, to give further stability and prevent movement along the line of the wall.

As regards the actual laying of the turves, experiment soon proved that the sods were not placed grass upwards, as had been popularly supposed,

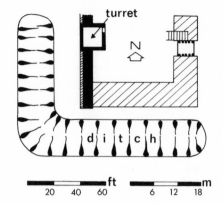

KEY

turf wall

milecastle gateway

stone wall

43 Plan of the replicas of Hadrian's Wall at Vindolanda. The Hadrianic Turf and Stone Walls were never joined in this manner, but limitations of space forced this arrangement on the builders

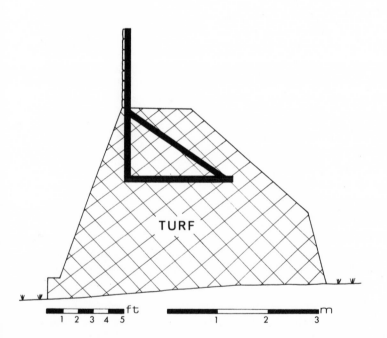

TURF

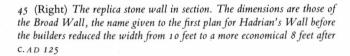

44 The replica turf wall in section. Experience gained since its construction suggests that the main vertical timbers should have been driven through the turf into the subsoil

45 (Right) The replica stone wall in section. The dimensions are those of the Broad Wall, the name given to the first plan for Hadrian's Wall before the builders reduced the width from 10 feet to a more economical 8 feet after c. AD 125

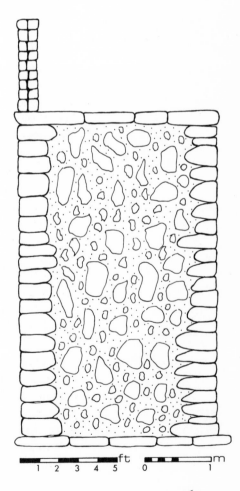

but grass downwards. Thus by using a spade to smooth down the uneven cuts it was simple to achieve a level surface after each layer had been laid. The physical problem of cutting the sods and conveying them to the site was in fact much greater than that of actually building the structure. Each turf, cut to the regulation Roman army dimensions of 18 inches by 12 inches by 6 inches, weighed approximately $2\frac{1}{4}$ stone. Les Turnbull calculated that the Romans would have needed some 1,400,000 turves weighing about 20,000 tons for each statute mile of the Turf Wall (and the parapet boarding alone would have required 53,000 feet of timber measuring 6 inches by 2 inches). The problems of transporting the turves from the quarries to the site were immense. Initially we constructed special two-man hods, but we soon found that experienced volunteers could carry the sods more speedily by hand. The site tended to become a quagmire in wet weather, and it was only through perseverance and hard work that the project came to be completed at all.

The stone wall

Fig. 45

The stone wall required less elaborate planning than the turf wall, once the decision had been taken to adopt the standard Broad Wall measurements. The major problem, again, was that of transporting the materials to the site. While we correctly anticipated the quantities of cut and faced stone necessary for the wall faces, we entirely underestimated the amount of rubble and concrete the inner core would consume. All told the 15 yards of wall needed 400 tons of stone, as did the turret (see below), and the whole of this 800 tons had to be brought from a demolished field wall nearby or as loose stones from the main excavations. Since we were unable to obtain lime mortar locally (an ironic fact, for this region was once a major exporter of lime), vast quantities of cement and sand also had to be imported from far afield, not to mention the water to mix them together with – our mason required about 800 gallons a day to keep him busy, which even with a tractor and jerry cans was a constant problem.

We learnt by experience as building progressed. It was essential, for instance, to keep the inner core of rubble and concrete higher than the outer faces at all times, for the core had to set hard before the mason could fill in the facing stones. In practical terms, this meant that the mason and one labourer could keep pace with five men filling in the core. As the wall grew higher we also needed two quite separate gangs on the two faces – separate personnel and separate supplies since communication between the two parties became increasingly difficult.

We decided to simulate Roman scaffolding when the wall reached a certain height, and accordingly dispatched our woodmen to a local pine forest to produce the necessary 30-feet-high uprights and all the cross-pieces. Tied together with rope and with sawn planks for foot-walks, the scaffolding proved simple to erect and perfectly stable. We had only just had time to make ourselves familiar with the quantities of timber required and the method of securing the framework to the rising stone wall, when we received word from a friendly building inspector that such scaffolding was now outlawed in Britain, and that we risked a heavy fine if it should be seen in use. Such are the pitfalls of replica construction!

Plate 83

Perhaps the most difficult policy decision we faced was where and which way up to position the chamfered stones which Major Joicey of Blenkinsopp Hall had kindly allowed us to use from the Wall at Walltown. Mr Charles Anderson, the former Department of the Environment foreman in charge of the conservation Wall gangs, considered that they might have been placed on the inner face of the Wall, acting as an inset a few feet above the ground; and there were many other suggestions. In the end, the stones were placed level with the rampart walk, jutting out slightly on the outside face, which seemed a tidy enough arrangement, although it is still not clear why they were used in the first place.

The design of the turf wall, therefore, occupied a great deal of time and thought and the stone wall much less. The construction of both replicas, however, demanded that practical considerations be kept to the fore, which sharpened the minds of the designers. Although our replicas were very short lengths of wall compared with the mighty sweep of Hadrian's Wall, it was possible to gain a real insight into the problems faced by the Roman army builders. For example, we considered carefully the logistics and time factor in our programme. Neither turf nor stone wall could be constructed during the winter months: the turf was too weak then, severe frosts ruled out cement work and the transport of materials to the site would have been impossible. The effective working season was therefore from April to mid-October, and we, like the Roman army, retired out of season to winter quarters to relax and recover our energy. So exhausted were we in fact after completing the walls in 1973 that we almost forgot that our plans, following Roman precedent, required a deep ditch on the forward side.

The ditch

Fig. 43

We soon discovered that the ditch-digging season was considerably shorter than the wall-building season, and – more valuably – that the ditch itself required as much time and labour as the construction of the turf wall (if one includes the quarrying of materials, the stone wall was much more expensive in both time and labour).

The ditch needed to be 30 feet wide and 10 feet deep. In Northumberland any ditch of this depth has to be cut through either solid rock, boulder clay or swamp, all of which the Roman ditch-diggers must have encountered. We were fortunate to have boulder clay only, but even so our workforce regarded the ditch-digging as the toughest part of the whole project. In dry weather boulder clay is almost as hard as rock; in wet weather it is like putty. Once the ditch is a few feet deep one has to cope not only with water from rain-storms but also with natural seepage through the sides, and if the water is not removed from the bottom of the trench it is impossible to work. By the same token, no man can dig a ditch 10 feet deep and 30 feet wide by sticking his spade into the ground and simply shovelling the material out: triple shovelling is required. Thus the man at the bottom shovels half way up the bank, where a second man transfers the spoil on to the top lip and a third spreads it out on to the glacis. Every so often glacial boulders are encountered, weighing up to a ton, and these must be split before removal – a relatively easy task if they are sandstone, a difficult one if they are whinstone.

The Roman mason and his centurion have always been admired for their work on the Wall, but equal if not greater credit should undoubtedly go to those who did not leave inscribed stones behind them – the men in the coal mines, sandpits, lime pits and quarries, the transport teams, the foresters and, last but not least, the unfortunate ditch-diggers.

The value of the replicas

Plate XV
Plate 84

In 1974 we completed the replicas by adding a typical Hadrian's Wall stone turret (based on the known dimensions of Brunton turret east of Chesters fort) and a timber milecastle gateway. Although the full significance of the project will emerge only after detailed analysis of the data collected and several years' observation of weathering processes, some points already stand out clearly.

The major problem the Romans must have faced, it transpires, was not the actual building of the Wall, for this required only a few trained men assisted by labourers: the crucial factor was that of supplies. In the first place raw materials – coal, limestone, sand, timber, iron and both faced and rubble sandstone – had to be obtained in vast quantities. Once these had been prepared, they then had to be transported, together with a large supply of water, to the numerous building sites, situated in some of the most difficult and inaccessible Northumbrian countryside. This must have involved the prior construction of metalled tracks, the assembly of far more vehicles and animals than the legions normally used and the setting up of elaborate administrative systems to cope with the far-flung detachments. In the construction process, therefore, for every ten men or so actually employed building the Wall at least ninety would have been required to maintain the supply of materials. Heavy summer rain must have halted or seriously disrupted work for weeks, while trouble in the lime pits would have slowed the Roman masons as much as a cement strike did ours.

The Vindolanda stone wall and turret have, not surprisingly, weathered little in the few years since they were built. The turf wall and the ditch, on the other hand, are showing signs of deterioration. The former has shrunk – over 14 inches at the highest point – and the outer face collapsed seriously in one place, because of the uneven drying of the turf on the most sheltered side. We learned from the Roman pre-Hadrianic rampart discovered nearby in 1973 how the problem could have been prevented and in June 1976 troops from the Royal Signals Junior Training Regiment added strengthening devices to the structure such as their counterparts nearly two millennia earlier had used: the base was given a stone platform, and brushwood and timber was laid horizontally in layers 2 feet apart to bind the rampart together. Informed guesses suggest that such a rampart ought to remain an effective wall for twenty years: we must wait and watch. The ditch has been silting up fast, and in one (admittedly very wet) season, the foot-deep drainage channel at the bottom was covered.

The educational value of these replicas is obvious to anyone who has seen them. There are academic arguments over the accuracy of particular details, which is inevitable when the greater part of the superstructure has had to be designed without the benefit of the Roman plans, but in general these walls do give people an idea of the majesty of Hadrian's Wall, enabling them to appreciate better the low-standing ruins on the Whin Sill a mile to the north of Vindolanda.

As a useful by-product it has also emerged that the nearby ancient remains are now easier to maintain and suffer far less casual damage than before. Young visitors work off their energies on the lofty replicas instead of the walls of headquarters building or *mansio*.

Much as we would like to construct further replicas – a stone milecastle for instance – we have little space left at Vindolanda that is not already occupied by buried or excavated Roman remains. Near Chesterholm Museum, however, there is a $\frac{3}{4}$-acre paddock, out of sight of the Roman fort and *vicus*, which would be ideal for a Romano-British native settlement. Such a settlement would show how the poorer contemporaries of the Vindolanda civilians actually lived, largely cut off from the wealth and influence of the frontier forts.

X The future at Vindolanda

The first six years' work at Vindolanda has been both rewarding and humiliating: we now know far more about the civilians on the frontier and the nature of the early, pre-Hadrianic garrisons than we did in 1970, but at the same time many of our preconceived ideas about frontier history have been destroyed, without being adequately replaced. Although the character and extent of the civilian occupation is now clear, we are left with the surprising information that that occupation was not continuous – and if it was not continuous, what caused the break(s), and where did the people go? Since there is no obvious political or military event yet known to us which would have brought about temporary abandonment, the implications of the Vindolanda evidence are of major importance to our understanding of the history of the north. That such a lack of continuity was not a special feature of Vindolanda alone has already been suggested by other archaeologists, who have suspected that similar hiatuses might have occurred at Birdoswald, Haltonchesters and Rudchester at the least; if this evidence is confirmed, our vision of the gradual consolidation of the region by peaceful development may be quite wrong. We must now search for explanations.

In spite of these break(s) in occupation, the civilians at Vindolanda can be seen as prosperous and numerous people, whose presence on the frontier transformed what would otherwise have been a tedious military existence. The majority of the *vicus* inhabitants were undoubtedly related to the soldiers in garrison, and therefore played a vital role in the maintenance of military morale and military recruitment. Equally important were the various civilian craftsmen whose products proved essential to the army commissariat: it was no surprise to detect the emergence at Vindolanda of metalworking in the later settlement, as demand and the availability of raw materials combined to create a minor industrial revolution – in an area which was not redeveloped until the late eighteenth century.

The early military occupation of the site has provided the most startling evidence in the past six years. The unusual chemistry of the soil has allowed us to examine living conditions on the pre-Hadrianic frontier in a detail which was both unexpected and deeply revealing. The nature of the environment, the use of flora and fauna, the construction techniques employed in wooden buildings, the crafts of leatherworking, weaving and woodworking are now much better known than they were before, and flesh has been added to the bare bones of the archaeological record. But the writing tablets are potentially the most important discovery at Vindolanda. Already they have revealed information about the diet of the troops and the movement of men and supplies, and much more will emerge as their translation continues. Equally significant will be the implications to be drawn from a study of the language in which the texts are written, for local Latin dialects and the assimilation of native words are branches of knowledge which have scarcely been explored as yet.

Vindolanda has much more to offer in the future, however. The first excavator, Anthony Hedley, believed that a small expenditure of time and manpower would uncover all the Roman remains: to-day, of course, there is a great deal more to archaeology than uncovering remains, while the work of the past few years has demonstrated that the site is much more complex than previously imagined. Total excavation of Vindolanda – that is, the complete examination of each successive layer of occupation, from the first settlement in the last decades of the first century to the effective abandonment some time in the fifth century – would involve a full-time labour force of twenty people and a time span of perhaps 100 years. It would also require a full-time team of specialists to work on the conservation of the finds and their interpretation, together with a Museum with display and storage space many times larger than anything to be found in the north of England. In some respects it is a daunting prospect, for the most complete picture of Vindolanda's history is beyond the reach of the present generation of archaeologists, but it does demonstrate how much knowledge of our past remains below the turf, and not only at Vindolanda. If one extended the calculations for Vindolanda to the frontier as a whole, one would readily appreciate that an army of archaeologists, with unlimited funds, would still be revealing new and important information after decades of continuous work.

Although the most pressing task now is the preparation of the research reports,[131] excavations on the site are still in progress. There are two priorities: the completion of work on the later civilian settlement and renewed study of the buildings within the later stone fort. As regards the *vicus*, work in the area between the military bath-house and the later fort wall has already revealed an extensive complex of metal-working establishments, with traces of both iron and bronze working: the major area still awaiting excavation is that to the west of *mansio* and bath-house, where one of Professor St Joseph's aerial photographs shows heavy concentrations of stone. Here, perhaps, there may lie a small temple complex, and beyond that there is room for either a rudimentary market-

Plate 5

place or more workshops and stores-buildings. When these areas have been completed we will be in a position to hazard a reasoned guess at the maximum population of the settlement in the later period. To the north of the Stanegate, the extensive cemeteries are at the moment safe from agricultural destruction, and one day, subject to the landowner's permission, a detailed examination of the remains will provide a valuable comparison with the work undertaken by Mr Peter Wenham at Trentholme Drive, York.

But the more urgent work lies within the walls of the later stone fort. The barrack buildings have never been examined, and excavation ought to provide the vital links between the troops and the civilians. We particularly need to know how soon the military establishment began to decline in both numbers and efficiency, and whether or not the soldiers were joined by some civilians inside the fort in the fourth century. This may prove a difficult matter to determine, for if the Wall garrison in the later fourth century was anything like that on the Danube, it will not be easy to distinguish between an unpaid, un-uniformed and largely peasant militia and the ordinary civilian. But the barracks at Vindolanda have probably been as little damaged by later activities as any on the Wall, and their examination will undoubtedly be a most rewarding task. After the barracks, the fort granaries are the next priority, for nothing shows the decline of orthodox Roman discipline more clearly than a granary, which was the first building to be turned over to additional accommodation when army discipline deteriorated. Eric Birley cut a trench across one of these buildings in 1935, and reported that occupation material similar to that in the barracks had been encountered.[132]

If the civilian settlement and the stone fort must take priority, further work on the pre-Hadrianic remains would produce the most dramatic results. Small-scale excavation will be attempted when money becomes available; the problem is that the sheer quantity of the finds makes the pre-Hadrianic research ten times as expensive as that on the later levels. The excavations of 1973–5 were possible only because first the *Observer* newspaper and then the author Hunter Davies gave us timely support, and because the Department of Pharmacy at Manchester University and BP Chemicals Ltd provided both the necessary technical knowledge for large-scale conservation and the expensive chemicals. There is little doubt that hundreds, and perhaps thousands, of writing tablets still lie amongst the remains of the early wooden forts, ready to yield invaluable information about the Stanegate frontier in the era before the construction of the Wall. It would, however, be foolhardy to exhume them without adequate financial provision for their treatment and elucidation.

Report writing and further excavation will, then, be the fundamental tasks of the next five years, although the Vindolanda Trust has other responsibilities which it must attend to, such as the schools courses and the fort of Carvoran both discussed in the appendix. Ultimately, however, the future is in the lap of the gods. Those of us who have worked at Vindolanda since 1970 hope that Moguntis, Maponus, the Veteres and the Genius of the Place are satisfied with our efforts so far – and that they will intercede on our behalf with Jupiter Optimus Maximus, so beloved of those in authority.

Appendix: The Vindolanda Trust

Aims

The Trust was founded in 1970 to pursue the following aims: the excavation of the Roman remains; their conservation for display to the public; the use of the site for training courses in archaeology for students; and the display of the finds in a good on-site museum. The excavations carried out since 1970 have already been described. In addition the Trust has furthered conservation by creating suitable laboratory facilities, and has improved the display of finds by purchasing Chesterholm as a museum in 1974 (it opened to the public in 1975, and is now the largest museum in the north devoted to Roman material). The most important work of the Trust, however, after the excavations, has been the training courses for schools.

Schools courses

The courses for schools in Romano-British history and archaeology were born of necessity, since the Trust could not afford to pay even modest expenses to volunteers over a long excavating season and needed to find some alternative form of labour. The courses have proved very worthwhile for the Trust: valuable research work has been undertaken, funds have been received, while the return of former pupils as volunteers during school holidays has ensured a constant supply of excavators of known ability. The benefits have been considerable for the pupils too: they have shared in the making of history, begun to understand something of the inter-disciplinary approach in archaeology and taken a pride in the creation of a centre of interest for the public. Every effort will be made to ensure that these courses continue in the future.

In addition, more varied schemes, which do not include excavation, are now being devised for pupils from a wider range of age groups. This opportunity for an expansion in our educational activities has arisen, paradoxically, because of the growth of unemployment. The government-backed agency for reducing unemployment, the Manpower Services Commission, has provided the finance for six newly qualified teachers to practise their skills for twelve months at Vindolanda and thereby to obtain invaluable experience of teaching history and archaeology. If the experiment is a success further such schemes may be introduced.

Carvoran

In 1971 the Trust purchased the 40-acre farm which contains the military and civilian remains of Carvoran, 8 miles to the west of Vindolanda. Although the acquisition of this property placed a severe strain upon finances it was thought to be a worthwhile sacrifice, for the site is an important one. As a former Stanegate frontier and later Wall site, its history should be similar to that of Vindolanda, thus providing an invaluable cross-check on chronology. It is also a very wet site – perhaps even worse than Vindolanda – and the early forts should therefore be exceptionally well preserved. But work here will not be started until the more pressing problems at Vindolanda have been solved and the research reports published.

Composition of the Vindolanda Trust

The composition of the Vindolanda Trust in 1970 and 1976 is listed below. A small charity of this nature leans very heavily upon the unpaid and part-time efforts of a large number of people, and increases in the size of the permanent staff usually place even more work upon the shoulders of invaluable volunteers, to whom we are very grateful.

The Vindolanda Trust 1970

TRUSTEES: Professor Eric Birley (Chairman), Brigadier Brian Archibald (Hon. Treasurer), Mrs Daphne Archibald (Hon. Secretary), Miss Elizabeth Archibald, Dr Anthony Birley, Mr Robin Birley, Dr Charles Bosanquet.

COMMITTEE OF MANAGEMENT: The Trustees, Dr John Mann.

The Vindolanda Trust 1976

TRUSTEES: Professor Eric Birley (Chairman), Miss Elizabeth Archibald, Professor Anthony Birley, Professor Barry Cunliffe, Dr Mark Hughes, Mr George Jobey, Major John Joicey, Professor Barri Jones, Dr John Mann, Professor John Wilkes.

COMMITTEE OF MANAGEMENT: The Trustees, Mr Geoffrey Hall, Mr David Hindley, Mr Denis Jones (Hon. Treasurer), Mr David Mawson (Hon. Solicitor), Mrs Mary Smith.

CO-OPTED MEMBERS (non-voting): Mr Robin Birley (Director), Mrs Patricia Birley (Curator), Mr Peter Bradley (Secretary), Dr Alan Bowman, Mr George Hodgson, Dr Mark Seaward, Dr David Thomas, Dr John Peter Wild.

Chronology

c. pre-90 ff.	Period I wooden fort (*c.* $3\frac{1}{2}$ acres)	
95–105	Periods IIa and IIb wooden forts (*c.* 8 acres)	⎫ Probable garrison
105–110	Period IIIa wooden fort (*c.* 8 acres)	⎬ First Cohort of
110–120	Period IIIb wooden fort (*c.* 8 acres)	⎪ Tungrians
120–125	Period IV wooden fort (*c.* 8 acres)	⎭
125–163	Vindolanda abandoned	
163	Construction of a new stone fort (*c.* $3\frac{1}{2}$ acres) perhaps by Fourth Cohort of Gauls. Start of civilian settlement (*vicus*) period I (enclosed area *c.* 2 acres)	
197	Alterations to the *vicus* and addition of defences	
245–270	Fort and *vicus* apparently abandoned	
270	Construction of a new stone fort ($3\frac{1}{2}$ acres) and period II *vicus* (*c.* 6–10 acres)	
350 ff.	Gradual abandonment of period II *vicus*	
370	Substantial repairs to the stone fort. Only limited occupation of *vicus* now	
400	Little serious military presence left at Vindolanda, although limited occupation of fort and *vicus* probably continues into fifth century and beyond	

Abbreviations

AA2, AA3, AA4	*Archaeologia Aeliana* (new series, 3rd series, 4th series)
AE	*L'Année Épigraphique* (Paris)
Arch. J.	*Archaeological Journal*
BAR	British Archaeological Reports
JRS	*Journal of Roman Studies*
RIB	R. G. Collingwood and R. P. Wright, *The Roman Inscriptions of Britain*, vol. i, Oxford 1965.

Chapter I

1 Stuart Piggott in I. A. Richmond (ed.), *Roman and Native in North Britain*, London 1958, 15.

2 R. E. M. Wheeler, *The Stanwick Fortifications*, Oxford 1954.

3 For a recent discussion of the evidence, see A. R. Birley, 'Petillius Cerealis and the Conquest of Brigantia', *Britannia*, iv (1973), 179–90.

4 Miss Dorothy Charlesworth was kind enough to show me round her fascinating excavations near Tullie House, Carlisle, in 1975, and my impression was that her pottery and bronzes pre-dated the earliest Vindolanda material by a number of years.

5 Tacitus, *Agricola*; see also the useful discussion in A. R. Burn, *Agricola and Roman Britain*, London 1953, and R. M. Ogilvie and I. A. Richmond (eds.), *Cornelius Tacitus, de Vita Iuli Agricolae*, Oxford 1967.

6 See James Curle's classic report, *A Roman Frontier post and its people*, London 1911, and B. R. Hartley, 'The Roman Occupation of Scotland: the evidence of Samian ware', *Britannia*, iii (1972), 1–55.

7 *Historia Augusta* (Hohl (ed.)), *Vita Hadriani*, 5, 2: *Brittanni teneri sub Romana dicione non poterant*.

8 *Vita Hadriani*, 11, 2.

9 See especially C. E. Stevens, 'The Building of Hadrian's Wall', *AA4*, xxvi (1948), 1–46.

10 A. R. Birley, 'Roman Frontiers and Roman Frontier Policy: some reflections on Roman Imperialism', *Durham and Northumberland Transactions*, iii (1970), 13–25, espec. 17.

11 As he kindly informed me in November 1975. This was detected by aerial photography in the exceptionally dry summer of 1975, and confirmed by trial excavation.

12 The case for abandonment at this time was established by Eric Birley, and his views are summarized in his *Research on Hadrian's Wall*, Kendal 1961, 185–7.

13 Rudyard Kipling, *Puck of Pook's Hill*, London 1907.

14 For the Antonine Wall in Scotland the best general summaries, with bibliographies, are Sir George Macdonald, *The Roman Wall in Scotland*, 2nd edn, Oxford 1934, and A. S. Robertson, *The Antonine Wall*, 4th edn, Glasgow 1970.

15 *RIB* 1700; see chapter IV.

16 For the Birdoswald evidence see J. J. Wilkes in *Britain and Rome*, Kendal 1966, 125, but also take into account the discovery of an altar dated between A D 276 and 282, in *JRS*, li (1961), 194 = *AE* 1962, 263, Coh. I *Aelia Dacorum Probiana* = A D 276–82. The claims for Haltonchesters and Rudchester have been made by Mr J. P. Gillam in lectures and discussions, and that for Wallsend by Mr C. M. Daniels during the excavations of 1975. Published accounts are awaited.

17 For the account of this extraordinary discovery, see John Clayton, 'The Temple of Coventina at Carrawburgh', *AA2*, viii (1880), 1–49.

18 R. C. Bosanquet in *AA2*, xxv (1904), 193–300; J. J. Wilkes in *AA4*, xxxviii (1960), 61–71, and *AA4*, xxxix (1961), 279–300 for the examination of a barrack block; Miss Dorothy Charlesworth in *AA5*, iii (1975), 17–42 for the commanding officer's residence. During the 1930s and in 1960–1 there were substantial excavations in the civilian settlement, reported in the relevant volumes of *AA4*.

19 Numerous excavation reports in *AA2*, between 1894 and 1897, and in *AA4*, ii (1926), 197–202 for the excavations of 1925, and by I. A. Richmond in *JRS*, xxx (1940), 161ff. for the excavations of 1939.

20 See John Hodgson's accounts in his *History of Northumberland*, part II, vol. iii, London 1840, 135–43, 204–6 and 292.

21 The long series of excavations at Birdos-

wald by F. G. Simpson, I. A. Richmond, Eric Birley and others provided the key to the chronology of the Wall accepted by most scholars until recently and by many even today. See Eric Birley, op. cit. (note 12), 196 for a full bibliography, but note especially the reports on the excavations of 1927–33.

22 See the invaluable Ordnance Survey *Map of Hadrian's Wall*, Chessington 1972.

Chapter II

23 In 1970 two important parts of the site lay outside the Trust's property: the major cemeteries lining the Stanegate road in the field to the north, and a fragment of the civilian settlement and the fort's rubbish dumps in another field to the south. This latter field was purchased by the Trust in 1971 through the good offices of Brigadier B. M. Archibald, and it was on this land that the extraordinarily rich early deposit was first discovered in 1972.

24 Tacitus, *Agricola*, chapters 17, 18, 20 and 22 (in particular).

25 Corbridge has produced the bulk of the information so far, Haltwhistle Burn fortlet and Vindolanda most of the remainder. See Eric Birley, op. cit. (note 12), 132–50.

26 This view now seems more likely with the discovery of a fort at Whickham by Dr N. McCord: see *Britannia*, ii (1970), 250.

27 See in particular C. E. Stevens, op. cit. (note 9).

28 Brenda Swinbank, *The Vallum Reconsidered*, Durham University Dissertation 1954.

29 The best summary of the evidence will be found in K. A. Steer, 'John Horsley and the Antonine Wall', *AA4*, xlii (1964), 1–40.

30 For a detailed examination of Severus' activities in Britain, see A. R. Birley, *Septimius Severus, the African Emperor*, London 1971.

31 By J. J. Wilkes (see note 18), and by J. P. Gillam and C. M. Daniels in 1975 (unpubl.).

32 By John Clayton in the mid-19th century (unpubl.).

33 See the report on the 1894 excavations in *AA2*, xvii (1895), pp. xxii–xxxii.

34 J. P. Gillam, in *AA5*, i (1973), 81–6.

35 Excavations were conducted at Wallsend in 1975 by Mr C. M. Daniels.

36 For civilian settlement in the frontier region generally see P. Salway, *The Frontier People of Roman Britain*, Cambridge 1965. For that on Hadrian's Wall see Robin Birley, *Civilians on the Roman Frontier*, Newcastle 1973.

37 For a summary of Mr George Jobey's invaluable work see 'Homesteads and Settlements of the Frontier area', in C. Thomas (ed.), *Rural Settlement in Roman Britain*, CBA Research Report 7, London 1966, 1–14, and numerous articles in *Archaeologia Aeliana*. See also Barri Jones and N. F. Higham in *Arch. J.* (forthcoming).

38 For the details of the forts and an extensive bibliography see Eric Birley, op. cit. (note 12), or J. Collingwood Bruce, *Handbook to the Roman Wall* (12th edn I. A. Richmond), Newcastle 1966.

39 Carvoran Farm was purchased by the Vindolanda Trust in 1972: see appendix.

40 Much of it was unrecorded, and the extent of the work must be guessed at after referring to various editions of J. Collingwood Bruce, *Handbook to the Roman Wall* (from 1851 onwards).

41 For an illuminating account of the construction of this road, popularly known as Wade's Road, see William Lawson, 'The Construction of the Military Road in Northumberland 1751–1757', *AA5*, i (1973), 177–93.

42 Christopher Hunter in *Philosophical Transactions*, xxiii (1702), 1131.

43 John Hodgson in op. cit. (note 20), 195–202.

44 I. A. Richmond and O. G. S. Crawford (eds.), 'The British Section of the Ravenna Cosmography', *Archaeologia*, lxxxix (1949), 1–50.

45 Op. cit. (note 42).

46 John Warburton, *Vallum Romanum*, London 1753.

47 For the value of John Horsley's work see especially Sir George Macdonald, 'John Horsley, scholar and gentleman', *AA4*, x (1933), 1–57.

48 John Wallis, *The Natural History and Antiquities of Northumberland*, vol. ii, London 1769, 24–31.

49 For an appreciation of Anthony Hedley, see Eric Birley, 'Anthony Hedley, a Centenary Memoir', *AA4*, viii (1931), 152–69.

50 John Hodgson, op. cit. (note 20), 195–202.

51 See Sir George Macdonald's later report, in *AA4*, viii (1931), 219–304.

52 See note 17.

53 See note 51.

54 See note 18.

55 See note 33.

56 *RIB* 1700.

57 See Eric Birley, op. cit. (note 12), 179, for a full bibliography.

58 See Robin Birley in *AA4*, xl (1962), 97–103.

59 *AA4*, xlviii (1970), 97–155.

Chapter III

60 Robin Birley, in *AA4*, xl (1962), 97–103 and *AA4*, xlviii (1970), 97–155.

61 Eric Birley and others in *AA4*, ix (1932), 222ff.; *AA4*, x (1933), 82ff.; *AA4*, xi (1934), 185ff.; and *AA4*, xii (1935), 204ff.

62 For Vindolanda, see Eric Birley's excavation reports: *AA4*, viii (1931), 182–212; *AA4*, ix (1932), 216–21; *AA4*, xii (1935), 218–57; *AA4*, xv (1938), 222–37; and *AA4*, xi (1934), 127–37 for the inscription to Caracalla. For a general statement of the chronology of the Wall, see the table in Eric Birley, op. cit. (note 12), facing p. 1.

63 For the reports on the military bath-houses, see the bibliography in Eric Birley, op. cit. (note 12) or J. Collingwood Bruce, op. cit. (note 38).

64 See especially Eric Birley in *AA4*, xii (1935), 204–59.

65 Cf. note 64.

66 Described and drawn in *AA4*, xlviii (1970), 106–8, and plan facing p. 112.

67 As Brigadier B. M. Archibald kindly informed me.

68 All the Vindolanda coins have been examined by Mr John Casey, at Durham University.

69 See John Wallis, op. cit. (note 48), 27.

70 John Hodgson, op. cit. (note 20), 197.

Chapter IV

71 R. E. Hooppell, *Vinovia*, London 1891.

72 The fullest description will be found in *Northumberland County History*, xiii (1930), 521–7, and 549–59.

73 See J. P. Gillam and I. MacIvor in *AA4*, xxxii (1954), 176–219.

74 See note 51 for the bath-house, and an aerial photograph by J. K. St Joseph, displayed in Chesters Museum, for the *mansio*.

75 For the bath-house, see J. Collingwood Bruce, *The Wall of Hadrian with especial reference to recent discoveries*, London 1874; for the Mithraeum see I. A. Richmond and J. P. Gillam, in *AA4*, xxix (1951), 1–92; and for Coventina's Well, note 17.

76 For comments about the unexcavated bath-house, see Eric Birley, op. cit. (note 12), 180; for the Mithraeum, John Hodgson in *AA1*, i (1882), 263–320; and for the temple to Mars Thincsus, Robin Birley in *AA4*, xxxix (1961), 216ff., and *AA4*, xl (1962), 97ff.

77 Great Chesters bath-house: J. Pattison Gibson and F. Gerald Simpson in *AA3*, v (1909), 158–67.

78 H. F. Pelham (ed.), *Arrian–Essays on Roman History*, Oxford 1911, ch. X.

79 See the surviving examples in *RIB*.

80 A report on some of the outstanding early finds can be found in Robin Birley, *AA5*, i (1973), 111–22.

81 Peter Wenham, *The Romano-British Cemetery at Trentholme Drive, York*, Chessington 1968.

82 See Robin Birley, op. cit. (note 80), 112–13.

83 See note 48.

84 Anne Ross, *Pagan Celtic Britain*, London 1967, 470.

85 See M. Henig, *The Vindolanda Jewellery*, Newcastle 1975, for general comments, and for particular gemstones see his reports in *A Corpus of Roman Engraved Gemstones from British sites*, 2 vols., BAR 8, Oxford 1974.

86 Eric Birley, *Roman Britain and the Roman Army*, Kendal 1953, 87–103.

87 *RIB*, p. 541.

88 See Mr George Hodgson's general statement in *The Vindolanda Animals*, Haltwhistle 1976.

89 Martin Henig, op. cit. (note 85).

90 But see J. P. C. Kent, 'Coin Evidence and the evacuation of Hadrian's Wall', in *Transactions of the Cumberland and Westmorland Antiquarian and Archaeological Society*, 2nd series, li (1952), 4–15.

91 *RIB* 899, 1616 and 1700; and *JRS*, xlvii (1957), 230.

Chapter V

92 John Hodgson, op. cit. (note 20), 195–202.

93 *RIB* 1685, *RIB* 1686 and *RIB* 1687.

94 Anthony Hedley in *AA1*, i (1822), 212.

95 Eric Birley in *AA4*, viii (1931), 202, note 29.
96 For a recent statement on the *Notitia* list, see M. W. C. Hassall in *Britannia*, iv (1973), 344–6, reviewing Dietrich Hoffmann, *Das Spätrömische Bewegungsheer und die Notitia Dignitatum*.
97 See S. S. Frere, *Britannia*, London 1967, 228–38.
98 Eric Birley analysed the travels of this regiment in *AA4*, viii (1931), 192–3.
99 Eric Birley and I. A. Richmond in *AA4*, xiii (1936), 221–33.
100 For the subsequent report on the bone and the wood, see Kathleen Blackburn in *AA4*, xlviii (1970), 145 for the wood, and 147–50 for the reports on the bone by Lionel Cowley and C. Bryner Jones.
101 *AA4*, xiii (1936), 232.
102 See J. Kewley in *AA5*, i (1973), 123–7.
103 Unpublished information from Eric Birley.
104 Eric Birley in *AA4*, xiii (1936), 138–41.
105 The late C. E. Stevens, whose provocative comments upon the history and archaeology of Hadrian's Wall did much to stimulate thought and discussion in the past forty years.
106 See Robin Birley in *AA4*, xlviii (1970), 102–6.

Chapter VI

107 Eric Birley in *AA4*, xii (1935), 241–2.
108 Robin Birley in *AA4*, xlviii (1970), 97–155.
109 Robin Birley in *AA4*, xl (1962), 97–103.

Chapter VII

110 See note 88.
111 Professor Barri Jones kindly organized this, and the specimen was examined by Dr Peter Gregory.
112 See M. R. D. Seaward, *The Vindolanda Environment*, Haltwhistle 1976, for a general discussion of the evidence. A more detailed discussion will be found in F. H. Perring (ed.), *The Biology of Bracken*, London 1976, which contains M. R. D. Seaward, 'Preliminary observations on the bracken component of the pre-Hadrianic deposits at Vindolanda, Northumberland'.
113 As Dr Antice Evans of Bangor University pointed out to me.
114 Anne Robertson, Margaret Scott and Lawrence Keppie, *Bar Hill: A Roman Fort and its Finds*, BAR 16, Oxford 1975.

115 Eric Birley in private correspondence: 'It is virtually certain that all commissioned officers, down to and including centurions, were legally entitled to be married, probably from the time of Augustus himself; that will explain the size of the flat for the centurion at the end of each barrack-block . . .'
116 Miss Dorothy Charlesworth kindly showed me photographs of two similar slippers from her excavations at Carlisle.
117 Mr J. P. Gillam drew my attention to the use of such footwear in Turkey.
118 See J. P. Wild, *Textile Manufacture in the Northern Roman Provinces*, Cambridge 1970, 89–122.
119 See R. P. Wright and others in *Britannia*, v (1974), 467, no. 44 and note 41.
120 By Dr Judith Turner at Durham University.

Chapter VIII

121 C. B. Welles, R. O. Fink, and J. F. Gilliam, *DURA-EUROPOS: Final Report*, vol. i: *The Parchments and Papyri*, New Haven 1959.
122 Robin Birley in *AA4*, xl (1960), 97–103.
123 At Chew Stoke, Somerset (in a well): see *JRS*, xlvi (1956), 115–18.
124 See A. K. Bowman and J. D Thomas, *The Vindolanda Writing Tablets*, Newcastle 1974, for a general description of the research.
125 See *Proceedings of the Cambridge Philological Society*, new series, xviii (1972).
126 A. K. Bowman and J. D. Thomas, op. cit. (note 124), 23.
127 A. K. Bowman, 'Roman Military Records from Vindolanda', *Britannia*, v (1974), 360–73.
128 For a general discussion see R. W. Davies, 'The Roman Military Diet', *Britannia*, ii (1971) 122–42.

Chapter IX

129 Cf. J. Collingwood Bruce, op. cit. (note 38), 12–19.
130 *Ibid.*, 17.

Chapter X

131 To be published by the Vindolanda Trust.
132 Unpublished information from Eric Birley.

Select bibliography

Eric Birley's *Research on Hadrian's Wall* (Kendal 1961) is the most comprehensive survey of the evidence for our knowledge of Hadrian's Wall, and contains the fullest bibliographies and references. It is now out of print, but libraries ought to have a copy. The twelfth edition of J. Collingwood Bruce's *Handbook to the Roman Wall* (Newcastle upon Tyne 1966) was extensively revised by Sir Ian Richmond before his death, and also contains a detailed bibliography. A. R. Birley's *Ninth Pilgrimage of Hadrian's Wall, 7–12 September 1969* (Kendal 1969) brings the bibliographies up to date. Excavation reports after that date will normally be found in recent volumes of *Archaeologia Aeliana*, 4th and 5th series, the annual volume of the Society of Antiquaries of Newcastle upon Tyne, and also in the *Transactions of the Cumberland and Westmorland Antiquarian and Archaeological Society*, 2nd series. Brief accounts of otherwise unpublished work may be found in the annual summaries printed now in *Britannia*, and formerly in *The Journal of Roman Studies*, published annually by the Roman Society.

General works

BIRLEY, A. R. *Life in Roman Britain*, London 1964.

BIRLEY, ERIC *Roman Britain and the Roman Army*, Kendal 1953.

BIRLEY, ROBIN *Civilians on the Roman Frontier*, Newcastle 1973.

COLLINGWOOD, R. G. and WRIGHT, R. P. *The Roman Inscriptions of Britain*, vol. i, Oxford 1965.

DAVIES, HUNTER *A Walk Along the Wall*, London 1974.

FRERE, S. S. *Britannia*, London 1967.

ORDNANCE SURVEY, H.M. *Map of Hadrian's Wall*, Chessington 1972.

RICHMOND, I. A. (ed.) *Roman and Native in North Britain*, London 1958.

—— *Roman Britain*, London 1963.

SALWAY, P. *The Frontier People of Roman Britain*, Cambridge 1965.

WILSON, R. J. A. *A Guide to the Roman Remains in Britain*, London 1975.

Works other than those given in the text and notes

BIRLEY, ERIC *The archaeology of the North of England*, Durham University, inaugural lecture 1958.

—— 'The Hinterland of Hadrian's Wall', *Durham and Northumberland Transactions*, xi (1958), 45–63.

—— 'Hadrian's Wall: some structural problems', *AA4*, xxxviii (1960), 39–60.

DOBSON, B. and BREEZE, D. 'Fort types as guides to garrisons: a reconsideration', in Eric Birley et al. (eds.), *Roman Frontier Studies 1969*, Cardiff 1974, 13–19.

HARTLEY, B. R. 'The Roman occupation of Scotland: the evidence of samian ware', *Britannia*, iii (1972), 1–55.

RICHMOND, I. A. 'The Romans in Redesdale', *Northumberland County History*, xv (1940), 63–154.

RIVET, A. L. F. 'The British Section of the Antonine Itinerary', *Britannia*, i (1970), 34–82.

List of illustrations

The author and publishers are grateful to Miss Alison Rutherford, Mr G. M. Young and the Department of Photography, University of Newcastle upon Tyne for the majority of the photographs; to Edwin Smith for plate 1; to Professor J. K. St Joseph and the Department of Aerial Photography, University of Cambridge, for plates 5 and 6; and to Professor Eric Birley for plates 48 and 49. The drawings are by Miss Louise Hird and Mrs Patricia Birley, adapted by Miss Charlotte Westbrook, except for: *fig. 1*, by Peter Bridgewater; *fig. 15*, after Eric Birley, *AA4*, xii (1935), plate xxii; *fig. 24*, after V. R. Abbott, *AA4*, xiii (1936), plate xx; and *fig. 42*, by Dr Alan Bowman.

Index